THE MOORHOUSE I. X. MILLAR LECTURE SERIES

A PROGRAM FOR MONETARY STABILITY

MILTON FRIEDMAN

THE MILLAR LECTURES · NUMBER THREE · 1959

FORDHAM UNIVERSITY PRESS · NEW YORK CITY

FOURTH PRINTING SEPT. · 1965

© FORDHAM UNIVERSITY PRESS · 1960
NEW YORK

LIBRARY OF CONGRESS CATALOG CARD NUMBER 60-9782

MANUFACTURED IN THE UNITED STATES OF AMERICA

Foreword

MONETARY PROBLEMS—a by-product of the indirect system of exchange —have long plagued the nations of the world. History is replete with instances in which such problems led not only to economic instability and uncertainty, but to political crises as well. In our own American experience there has hardly been a period when the economy was not beset by one type of monetary ill or another.

Consider, for example, the more important monetary disturbances of our own time, viz., those of the last 30 years or so. Our legacy from the financial collapse of 1929 was a monetary and banking system which was virtually defunct. Though some progress was made in shoring up our monetary and banking institutions after 1933, this of itself was inadequate to help us escape the deflation and mass unemployment which persisted throughout the 1930's.

For the decade of the 1940's, of course, the pendulum swung to the other side of the arc. Following the outbreak of World War II, and particularly after our direct involvement in 1941, an attempt was made to hold the line against inflation. This attempt achieved at best only partial success. Support by the Federal Reserve System of the prices of government securities, wartime military expenditures, the postwar investment boom, and the postwar pent-up demand for consumer goods backed by liquid assets acquired during the War combined to produce a rise in prices throughout the War and early postwar period.

Although inflation subsided somewhat after 1948, it was intensified by the outbreak of hostilities in Korea in the period after 1950. During the latter part of 1953, and throughout 1954 and 1955, prices remained relatively stable. But in 1956, the inflationary rise received a new stimulus. Caused largely by another investment boom, the inflationary movement had such momentum that it caused prices to rise even in the face of the 1957-1958 recession.

Professor Friedman's objective in this third of the Moorhouse I. X. Millar Lecture Series is certainly not one of finding a formula which will eradicate all uncertainty and instability attending monetary disturbances. For these, as he puts it, are "unavoidable concomitants of progress and change." However, it is possible to attenuate further the amplitude of our fluctuations by modifying, and in some cases completely revamping the monetary and banking arrangements currently in force in the United States. Specifically, this is the task to which Professor Friedman addresses himself.

For many years it was believed that money was a purely passive agent, unable of itself to exert any appreciable influence over the course of economic events. But all this has changed, and today it is widely recognized that money does matter in shaping the economic well-being of nations. If price stability, full employment, balanced economic growth and all of the other economic desiderata are to be achieved, it is imperative that our monetary and banking mechanism be made to operate consistently with the attainment of these objectives.

Any discussion of monetary and banking reform, Professor Friedman believes, must define the role to be played by government—"the restrictions it should impose on private individuals, the powers that should be granted to governmental authorities, and the criteria that should guide the use of these powers." Any attempt to reform our present-day monetary and banking arrangements must be based upon a thorough understanding of the government's reasons for operating in this sector in the first place, its objectives and its record of accomplishments. Each of these elements is given serious consideration.

A number of interesting proposals for reforming the monetary instruments currently to be found in the tool bag of the Federal Reserve System are introduced and supported with extremely cogent arguments. One of the more radical of these recommendations is that the Federal Reserve authorities abandon two of their quantitative control instruments—rediscounting and variation of legal reserve requirements.

Federal open market operations, Professor Friedman believes, are entirely adequate to regulate the money supply. In his estimate, the variable in terms of which Federal Reserve policy should be formulated is the stock of money, rather than the level of interest rates. Control over interest rates, he feels, is beyond the purview and control of the monetary authorities. If this premise be admitted, then it is not difficult to appreciate his position, because both rediscounting and variation of legal reserve requirements are, as he puts it, "technically poor instruments for controlling the supply of money." This as well as many other issues raised in his book are likely to incite considerable controversy both in and out of professional economic circles.

In developing his arguments for monetary and banking reforms, Professor Friedman writes lucidly, forcefully and with a conviction which stems, undoubtedly, from his ability to perceive and analyze monetary and banking problems in a way that few present-day students of economics can. Whether the proposals advanced by him will be implemented, either in whole or in part, cannot, of course, be foretold. But if they are not, it certainly will not be due to any lack of consistency or logical flaws in his reasoning. On this point, if no other, all readers of this enlightening and challenging work will remain agreed.

JOSEPH R. CAMMAROSANO
*Department of Political Philosophy
and Social Sciences*

*December, 1959
Fordham University*

Prefatory Note

THIS BOOK CONSISTS OF A slightly revised and expanded version of the Moorhouse I. X. Millar Lectures that I had the honor to give at Fordham University in October 1959. The suggestions for monetary reform it contains, and even more, the evidence adduced in support of them, are largely a by-product of my recent research in the field of money: a large-scale study, now nearly complete, of the secular and cyclical behavior of the money supply in the United States on which I have been collaborating with Mrs. Anna J. Schwartz under the auspices of the National Bureau of Economic Research, and a variety of research projects in the same general area on which I have been cooperating with members of the Workshop in Money and Banking of the University of Chicago. Although I owe much to those with whom I have worked in this research, none bears any responsibility for the policy views expressed herein.

I owe a heavy debt to Mrs. Schwartz. In addition to her contribution to the basic research, she checked details for accuracy, corrected errors in my early drafts, and made numerous helpful suggestions on broader matters of both content and organization. I have benefitted also from comments on early drafts by my wife, Rose Director Friedman, and by a number of other friends, including Gary Becker, Arthur F. Burns, John Deaver, Aaron Director, Harry G. Johnson, Reuben Kessel, David Meiselman, and George J. Stigler. The discussions following the lectures at Fordham and at several sessions of the Workshop in Money and Banking were highly useful in guiding the final revisions made in preparing the lectures as delivered for publication. I am indebted also to Mark Wehle and Tom Teng-Pin Yu of the National Bureau of Economic Research for computational and other assistance, to Irving Forman, also of the National Bureau, for preparing the Chart in Chapter I, and to Alyce Monroe and Sondra Sward of the University of Chicago for secretarial assistance above and beyond the call of duty.

The fine hand of William T. Hogan, S.J., smoothed every difficulty in connection with the delivery of the lectures. His thoughtfulness and thoroughness from the initial extension of the invitation to deliver the lectures to their completion left me only one problem: what to say. Miss Emily Schossberger and Edwin A. Quain, S.J., of the Fordham University Press have been equally helpful in the publication of the lectures. I am much indebted to all three.

MILTON FRIEDMAN

December 16, 1959
University of Chicago

Table of Contents

A PROGRAM FOR MONETARY STABILITY

Chapter One

The Background of Monetary Policy

THE PAST THREE DECADES have seen first a sweeping revolution against previously accepted economic thought about the role of monetary factors in economic change and then a counterrevolution that is still incomplete but promises to be no less sweeping. Before the great depression of the early 1930's, accepted economic doctrine attached great importance to the stock of money as a determinant of the level of money income and of the price level. The great depression spawned a revolution in ideas. Though, on a retrospective examination, the depression is a tragic testimonial to the potency of monetary factors—the stock of money fell by a third from 1929 to 1933—the failure of the monetary authorities to stem the depression was taken as evidence that they could not have done so. The view became widespread that "money does not matter," that the stock of money is a purely passive concomitant of economic change and plays no independent part except as it may affect a limited range of market interest rates, themselves of minor significance. Hence the only role assigned monetary policy was to keep whatever interest rates it affected low so as to avoid interfering with the investment regarded as needed to offset the secular stagnation that was confidently expected to be the major problem for the future.[1]

Two forces combined to produce a counterrevolution in ideas. One was strictly academic—scholarly criticism and analysis of the ideas of John Maynard Keynes, the chief architect of the intellectual revolution. The other, and more obvious, though perhaps not more important, was

the brute force of events. Many countries in the postwar period, including the United States, pursued "cheap-money" policies. Every such
country experienced either open inflation or a network of partly effective,
partly ineffective, controls designed to suppress the inflationary pressure.
In every case, the stock of money rose as a result of the cheap-money
policies and so did prices, either openly or in whatever disguise was most
effective in circumventing the controls. No country succeeded in stemming inflation without adopting measures directed at restraining the
growth of the stock of money. And every country that did hold down
the growth of the stock of money succeeded in checking the price rise.
Western Germany's "economic miracle" after the monetary reform of
1948 was the most dramatic episode, but the experience of Italy, of
Great Britain, and of the United States differed only in detail. And
French experience, prior to the monetary reforms at the end of 1958,
is equally striking testimony by its contrast in both policy and outcome.

These developments in the world of scholarship and of affairs have
produced a rebirth of interest in monetary changes. It is by now clear,
and widely accepted, that money does matter and matters very much.
There has been an increasing amount of research by economists during
recent years on just how monetary forces operate. There has also been
an increasing amount of attention devoted by public and quasi-public
groups to the problems of monetary policy. Within the past decade, there
have been two extensive Congressional investigations concerned exclusively with monetary policy—the Douglas and Patman investigations [2]—
and Congressional investigations of price stability, economic growth, and
the like have directed extensive attention to monetary problems—notably the Flanders, Byrd, and later Douglas and Patman investigations.[3]
The American Assembly recently devoted one of its sessions to United
States monetary policy.[4] The Committee for Economic Development,
with financial assistance from the Ford Foundation, has launched a
Commission on Money and Credit that is engaged in a sweeping investigation and analysis of our monetary arrangements. One must go back
half a century, to the years following the panic of 1907, to find a comparable degree of public interest in the structure of our monetary
institutions.

In this book I shall present a series of suggestions for reforming the
monetary arrangements of this country. In venturing suggestions on so
broad a scale, an individual cannot possibly be so judicious, so cognizant
of the many detailed aspects of policy, so sensitive to conflicting interests

as a Commission composed of representatives of the many important groups in the community affected by monetary arrangements. To counterbalance these serious defects, he has the advantage that he need not compromise and hence can be more radical—in the etymological sense of going to the roots of the matter—more consistent, and more venturesome.

In proposing measures of reform, one can accept the general structure of present monetary and banking arrangements, and analyze possibilities of improving them in detail. Alternatively, one can re-examine the general structure itself and propose, if that seems desirable, its reformation. It so happens that the order in which it seemed on other grounds desirable to examine various issues corresponds roughly to a progression from detailed to more sweeping reform. In the next chapter, I shall examine the tools of Federal Reserve policy—the means whereby the Federal Reserve System carries out whatever policy goals it may be pursuing; in the third chapter, I shall examine debt management and banking reform. The proposals under each of these headings are independent in the sense that they are separately desirable whatever else is done or if nothing else is done, though the proposals for banking reform do involve a radical reshaping of the banking structure. In the concluding chapter, I shall turn to the criteria of monetary policy, which is to say, the use to be made of the tools and the banking structure previously discussed. This topic is inseparable from international monetary arrangements, which are therefore also examined in the last chapter. My proposals about criteria are in their turn independent of the proposals about tools. They are desirable even if the present antiquated kit of tools is retained, though of course, they might be expected to produce superior results with improved means for putting them into effect.

The central problem in respect to monetary and banking arrangements is the role government should play—the restrictions it should impose on private individuals, the powers that should be granted to governmental authorities, and the criteria that should guide the use of these powers. Proposals for reforming these arrangements must rest implicitly or explicitly on two pillars: first, a conception of the reasons why government should be concerned with this area of economic activity and the objectives to be achieved through government intervention; second, some understanding of previous experience with government intervention. The rest of this chapter is devoted to these topics. In the limited space available, I can hope at best to be suggestive rather than exhaustive.

WHY SHOULD GOVERNMENT INTERVENE IN MONETARY AND BANKING QUESTIONS?

The point of view from which I shall examine the role of government in monetary matters is that of a liberal in its original sense—a viewpoint that I used to call nineteenth-century liberalism but that, in the light of changing currents of thought, I am now beginning, perhaps too hopefully, to call the "new liberalism." Such a liberal regards the market as the only means so far discovered of enabling individuals to coordinate their economic activities without coercion. He recognizes that government has an important role to play, but is suspicious of assigning to government any functions that can be performed through the market, both because this substitutes coercion for voluntary cooperation in the area in question and because, by giving government an increased role, it threatens freedom in other areas. Control over monetary and banking arrangements is a particularly dangerous power to entrust to government because of its far reaching effects on economic activity at large—as numerous episodes from ancient times to the present and over the whole of the globe tragically demonstrate. In consequence, one question that a liberal must answer is whether monetary and banking arrangements cannot be left to the market, subject only to the general rules applying to all other economic activity.

I am by no means certain that the answer is indubitably in the negative. What is clear is that monetary arrangements have seldom been left entirely to the market, even in societies following a thoroughly liberal policy in other respects, and that there are good reasons why this should have been the case.

These reasons can perhaps be elucidated best by considering the operation of a pure commodity standard, which at first sight seems to require no government intervention. Let us conceive of a modern society in which all money consists exclusively of physical units of a commodity or literal warehouse receipts for the commodity. The commodity in question might be gold or silver or copper or bricks or some combination of these or of other goods in fixed proportions, as under any of the variety of symmetallic or commodity reserve standards that have been proposed. The amount of the commodity in use as money would depend on its cost of production relative to other goods, and on the fraction of their wealth people want to hold in the form of money; additions to the stock of money could come from production by private enterprise; changes in the rate of production would reflect changes in the relative value placed on the monetary commodity and other goods or in the relative costs of producing the one and the other.[5] Large changes in the stock of money would be unlikely to occur over short periods, hence such a standard would provide a reasonably stable monetary framework and would not itself be a source of short-run instability. In practice, when standards remotely approaching this ideal have prevailed, government has frequently been assigned or has assumed the function of stamping the weight or fineness of the metal, and, of course, has not infrequently used its position to acquire resources through "sweating" and similar devices. There is no need, however, for government to assume even this function any more than it need now assume responsibility for certifying the weight and fineness of metals used in commercial trade—the "Good Housekeeping" seal is strictly private.

The maintenance of a commodity standard requires the use of real resources to produce additional amounts of the monetary commodity— of men and other resources to dig gold or silver or copper out of the ground or to produce whatever other commodities constitute the standard. In a stationary economy, production is needed solely to make good losses through wear and tear; in a growing economy, also to provide for an increase in the stock of money. Interestingly enough, the amount of resources required to provide for growth does not depend on the commodity or commodities used as the standard but only on the cash balance preferences of the public and on the rate of growth of the economy. The amount required is by no means negligible—for example, under a pure commodity standard, the United States would at present be devoting about 2½% of its national product or about $8 billion a year to produce directly or indirectly through foreign trade additional amounts of the monetary commodity to add to the amounts already in circulation or in warehouses.[6]

The use of so large a volume of resources for this purpose establishes a strong social incentive in a growing economy to find cheaper ways to provide a medium of exchange. This incentive is reinforced by the private incentive that would be present even in a stationary economy using a permanent and indestructible commodity, so that maintenance of the standard required no continuing production. Each individual separately must give up real resources to acquire money and, conversely, he can get real resources by parting with money. Hence, he can gain if he can find a cheaper way to provide a medium of exchange. The obvious way, and the one that developed historically, is to introduce fiduciary elements into the monetary system. Private promises to pay the monetary commodity are as good as the monetary commodity itself—so long as they command wide confidence that they will be fulfilled—and far cheaper to produce, since the issuers can meet possible demands for redemption by keeping on hand an amount of the monetary commodity equal to only a fraction of their outstanding promises. A pure commodity standard therefore tends to break down.

The introduction of fiduciary elements would not require government intervention if such promises to pay were always fulfilled, or, alternatively, if the community were willing to carry to the extreme the doctrine of *caveat emptor*. But the first is not likely to occur, and the second neither is likely to occur nor is it clear that it would be desirable if it did. What is involved is essentially the enforcement of contracts, if the failure of an issuer to fulfill his promise is in good faith, or the prevention of fraud, essentially of counterfeiting, if it is not. Both are functions that most liberals would wish the state to undertake. It so happens that the contracts in question are peculiarly difficult to enforce and fraud peculiarly difficult to prevent. The very performance of its central function requires money to be generally acceptable and to pass from hand to hand. As a result, individuals may be led to enter into contracts with persons far removed in space and acquaintance, and a long period may elapse between the issue of a promise and the demand for its fulfillment. In fraud as in other activities, opportunities for profit are not likely to go unexploited. A fiduciary currency ostensibly convertible into the monetary commodity is therefore likely to be overissued from time to time and convertibility is likely to become impossible. Historically, this is what happened under so-called "free banking" in the United States and under similar circumstances in other countries. Moreover, the pervasive character of the monetary nexus means that the failure of an issuer to fulfill his promises to pay has important effects on persons other than either the issuer or those who entered into a contract with him in the first instance or those who hold his promises. One failure triggers others, and may give rise to widespread effects. These third-party effects give special urgency to the prevention of fraud in respect of promises to pay a monetary commodity and the enforcement of such contracts.

These difficulties with a money consisting of a mixture of commodity and fiduciary elements may seem resolvable by a further transition to a purely fiduciary currency issued by private parties. Such a currency would involve a negligible use of real resources to produce the medium of exchange and would therefore seem to avoid any pressure to undermine it arising from the possibility of saving real resources. This is true for the community as a whole but not for any single issuer of currency. So long as the fiduciary currency has a market value greater than its cost of production—which under favorable conditions can be compressed close to the cost of the paper on which it is printed—any individual issuer has an incentive to issue additional amounts. A fiduciary currency would thus probably tend through increased issue to degenerate into a commodity currency—into a literal paper standard—there being no stable equilibrium price level short of that at which the money value of currency is no greater than that of the paper it contains. And in view of the negligible cost of adding zeros, it is not clear that there is any finite price level for which this is the case.

This analysis, then, leads to the conclusion that some external limit must be placed on the volume of a fiduciary currency in order to maintain its value. Competition does not provide an effective limit, since the value of the promise to pay, if the currency is to remain fiduciary, must be kept higher than the cost of producing additional units. The production of a fiduciary currency is, as it were, a technical monopoly, and hence, there is no such presumption in favor of the private market as there is when competition is feasible.

Incidentally, it is a monopoly that so far as I know has a unique property—the total value to the community of the stock of the monopoly product is entirely independent of the number of units in the stock. For any other item entering into economic exchange that I can think of, be it shoes or hats or tables or houses or even honorific titles, the aggregate value of the stock in terms of other goods depends on the number of units in it, at least outside some limits. For money, it does not. If there are five million pieces of paper, or five thousand, or five hundred million, as long as the number is relatively stable, the aggregate value is the same; the only effect is that each unit separately has a smaller or larger value as the case may be; that is, prices expressed in terms of the money are higher or lower.

These, then, are the features of money that justify government intervention: the resource cost of a pure commodity currency and hence its tendency to become partly fiduciary; the peculiar difficulty of enforcing contracts involving promises to pay that serve as a medium of exchange and of preventing fraud in respect to them; the technical monopoly character of a pure fiduciary currency which makes essential the setting of some external limit on its amount; and, finally, the pervasive character of money which means that the issuance of money has important effects on parties other than those directly involved and gives special importance to the preceding features. Something like a moderately stable monetary framework seems an essential prerequisite for the effective operation of a private market economy. It is dubious that the market can by itself provide such a framework. Hence, the function of providing one is an essential governmental function on a par with the provision of a stable legal framework.

The central tasks for government are also clear: to set an external limit to the amount of money and to prevent counterfeiting, broadly conceived. To accomplish the first, governments have specified the use of a particular commodity as a currency, established or accepted central banks, and imposed restrictions on who may issue promises to pay the basic money and on what terms; to accomplish the second, governments have not only used ordinary police measures but also have assumed for themselves a monopoly of issue of certain kinds of money, have regulated banks and other issuers of money, and have supervised their operation.

The appropriateness of governmental responsibility for the monetary system has of course been long and widely recognized. For the United States, it is explicitly provided for in the constitutional provision which gives Congress the power "to coin money, regulate the value thereof, and of foreign coin." There is probably no other area of economic activity with respect to which government intervention has been so uniformly accepted. This habitual and by now almost unthinking acceptance of governmental responsibility makes thorough understanding of the grounds for such responsibility all the more necessary, since it enhances the danger that the scope of government intervention will spread from activities that are to those that are not appropriate in a free society, from providing a monetary framework to determining the allocation of resources among individuals.

Given that some responsibility for monetary matters has been assigned to the government of the United States since its creation, how has this responsibility been discharged? What in fact is the background of experience with governmental intervention in monetary matters?

THE HISTORICAL BACKGROUND

The Great Depression did much to instill and reinforce the now widely held view that inherent instability of a private market economy has been responsible for the major periods of economic distress experienced by the United States. On this view, only a vigilant government, offsetting continuously the vagaries of the private economy, has prevented or can prevent such periods of instability. As I read the historical record, I draw almost the opposite conclusion. In almost every instance, major instability in the United States has been produced or, at the very least, greatly intensified by monetary instability. Monetary instability in its turn has generally arisen either from governmental intervention or from controversy about what governmental monetary policy should be. The failure of government to provide a stable monetary framework has thus been a major if not the major factor accounting for our really severe inflations and depressions. Perhaps the most remarkable feature of the record is the adaptability and flexibility that the private economy has so frequently shown under such extreme provocation.

A brief sketch of some highlights of our monetary experience may illustrate this thesis; it cannot of course prove it.[7]

The thesis is almost self-evident for the major inflations of our history. These have all been associated with war and were quite clearly produced by the use of the printing press or its equivalent to finance governmental expenditures. This is true of the Revolutionary War inflation, which made "continental" a synonym for worthlessness, and of the sizable increases in prices during the War of 1812, the Civil War, World War I, and World War II. In none of these wars, including the Revolution, was the use of the printing press necessarily unwise, given the alternatives available to the policy makers at the time. What is relevant for my thesis, however, is not the wisdom of the policy followed but the fact that the price rises and associated economic disturbances were in large measure clearly attributable to governmental action in financing its expenditures and controlling the money supply.

The major contractions or depressions require more attention. The most notable of them prior to the establishment of the Federal Reserve

System were (1) the depressed period of the late 1830's and early 1840's; (2) the contraction from 1873–79; (3) the mid-1890's; and (4) the contraction of 1907–08. In each case monetary factors played a critical role.

THE PERIOD FROM 1837 TO 1843

The banking panic of 1837 was followed by exceedingly disturbed economic conditions and a long contraction to 1843 that was interrupted only by a brief recovery from 1838 to 1839. This Great Depression is particularly interesting for our purposes. It is the only depression on record comparable in severity and scope to the Great Depression of the 1930's, and its monetary concomitants largely duplicate those of its later mate. In both, a substantial fraction of the banks in the United States went out of existence through suspension or merger —around one quarter in the earlier and over one-third in the later contraction—and the stock of money fell by about one-third. There is no other contraction that even closely approaches this dismal record. In both cases, erratic or unwise governmental policy with respect to money played an important part.

In the earlier period, the chartering of the Second Bank of the United States in 1816 and then the failure to renew its charter when it expired in 1836 after the Bank War in which Andrew Jackson and Nicholas Biddle were the chief protagonists, set the stage for the subsequent monetary difficulties. The Bank contracted sharply prior to the termination of its federal charter. After the lapsing of the federal charter, Biddle continued the bank under a Pennsylvania charter and there was a rebound which preceded the 1837 panic. Not long thereafter he embarked on his project of supporting the world price of cotton to bolster the American economy.[8] This venture fostered a sizable increase in the stock of money, accompanied by the brief expansion of 1838 to 1839, at a time when world-wide deflation called for a decrease in a country on a metallic standard. This world-wide movement would almost certainly have meant a sizable contraction in the United States in any event. But the result of internal monetary difficulties was to make the decline, when it came after the resounding failure of the Bank in 1839, much more severe than it need have been.[9] The effects of the operations by the Bank in producing monetary uncertainty were intensified by the successive financial measures adopted by the government after the lapsing of the bank charter—the Deposit Act calling for the distribution of the surplus, the Specie Circular, and the establishment of an Independent Treasury in 1840 and its repeal the next year.

THE CONTRACTION OF 1873–79

The Civil War greenback inflation involved the suspension of convertibility of greenbacks into gold early in 1862. From then until the resumption of gold payments in 1879, the U.S. was on an inconvertible paper standard. The exchange rate between the greenback dollar and other currencies was determined in private markets and fluctuated from day to day—as is the case today with the Canadian dollar.

A major aim of policy at the time was to resume gold payments at the pre-war exchange rate. Since world prices were roughly stable or falling, the achievement of this aim required that prices in the United States fall to less than half their level at the price peak in 1865. This is precisely what happened by 1879. Despite the official policy, the price fall was not produced by a reduction in the quantity of money. The most that governmental measures were able to achieve was to keep the money supply from expanding sharply. But this was enough. The economy was growing so rapidly that some increase in the money supply was associated with a halving of prices in fourteen years.

The price fall did not occur evenly during the period. Most of the fall came from 1873 to 1879, a period of economic contraction and of declining capital inflows from abroad. It was likewise a period when the money supply fell a trifle. Though concentration on money rather than real magnitudes has caused this contraction to be adjudged even more severe than it actually was, it was nevertheless one of the longest and more severe on record. Yet the remarkable feature of this period is that so sharp a price decline did not produce an even sharper decline in output. That it did not is a tribute to the underlying strength of the forces making for expansion and to the flexibility of prices and wages.[10]

THE 1890's

The rapid boom that followed resumption and that was fostered by unprecedented harvests and favorable balances of payments was succeeded by a reaction, and then by relative stability. This was a period of declining world prices as a result of a declining rate of growth in gold output and the adoption of the gold standard by a widening number of countries, of which the United States was one of the more important. The downward pressure on nominal prices was accompanied by rapid economic growth. Nonetheless, it stimulated a political demand for monetary expansion which joined with the interests of Western mining states to produce agitation for the free coinage of silver. From the first victory of the silver forces in the Bland-Allison Act of 1878 to sometime after Bryan's defeat in 1896, the "money" question was the major political issue of the time, reaching its emotional zenith with Bryan's famous "Cross of Gold" speech accepting the Democratic nomination for President.

The accelerated rate of decline of prices abroad required domestic readjustments in any event after 1890. As it was, the agitation over silver and the close approach to victory of the "free silver" forces greatly intensified the difficulties. They created a lack of confidence both at home and abroad in the maintenance of the gold standard that led to something of a "flight" from the dollar—or rather a series of flights and returns as the strength of the free silver forces fluctuated. The United States experience of this period is very similar to the British exchange crises after World War II. In both cases, a government was seeking to maintain a fixed exchange rate. In both cases, the ability of the government to do so was uncertain. In both cases, it was clear that if there was any change, it would be a depreciation of the relevant currency. Hence in both cases there was an incentive for holders of money to reduce balances held in the currency in question, an incentive that varied in intensity with the likelihood that the government would succeed. In both cases, the shift in incentives produced rapid fluctuations in short-term balances and serious economic disturbances.

Of course there were also important differences: in Britain, the uncertainty did not hinge directly on the outcome of a political contest; the commitment of Britain to full employment gave it much less leeway in domestic monetary policy; the development of direct exchange and trade controls gave it means of affecting its balance of payments other than through movements in prices and incomes; foreign trade was of greater relative importance to Britain; and, finally, Britain did devalue.

For the U.S. in the 1890's, the economic disturbances were manifested in a severe banking panic and the suspension of convertibility of deposits into currency in 1893, and a highly depressed period from early 1893 to mid-1897, interrupted only by a brief cyclical revival from June 1894 to December 1895, one of the few revivals in our history in which per capita output did not reach its level at the preceding cyclical peak.

In retrospect, it seems clear that early and firm acceptance of either of the two policies over which the controversy raged—either a firm and unquestioned commitment to gold or an equally firm and unquestioned commitment to silver—would have avoided a large part of the economic difficulties of the period. What was damaging was the uncertainty about which policy would be followed.

The final defeat of Bryan and the silver forces was achieved not by domestic political agitation or the Republican victory in 1896, but by the discovery of commercially feasible means to apply the cyanide process to the extraction of gold from the low-grade ores of South Africa and by the roughly simultaneous gold discoveries in Alaska and elsewhere. The resulting flood of gold produced the price inflation that Bryan and his followers had wanted to achieve with silver. From 1896 to 1913 wholesale prices in the United States rose by 50 per cent.

THE CONTRACTION OF 1907–08

The only major contraction during this period was the contraction of 1907–08, which was accompanied and intensified by the banking panic of 1907 and by the associated suspension of convertibility of bank deposits into currency. Though relatively brief, the contraction was severe. Among all those we have surveyed and still shall survey, this is the one severe contraction in which neither governmental monetary action nor controversy over what governmental policy should be played a clear and direct role. True enough, the Treasury, particularly under Secretary Shaw, had been assuming a wider range of central banking activities and had been intervening frequently through open market operations or their equivalent to smooth financial difficulties, and these activities had encouraged banks to reduce reserves relative to liabilities. But there was no direct link between these Treasury activities and the contraction, as there was between the Bank War and the contractions of 1837–38 and 1839–43, or between resumption policies and the contraction of 1873–79, or between the silver agitation and the depressed conditions of 1893–97.

The banking panic of 1907 contributed to renewed public interest in banking reform, and to the establishment of the National Monetary Commission, which issued its monumental special studies in 1910. The result was the enactment of the Federal Reserve Act in 1913.

UNDER THE FEDERAL RESERVE SYSTEM

The establishment of the Federal Reserve System was the most notable change in our monetary institutions since at least the Civil War National Banking Act. For the first time since the Second Bank of the United States, it established a separate official body charged with explicit responsibility for monetary conditions and supposedly clothed with adequate power to achieve monetary stability or, at least, to prevent pronounced instability. It is therefore instructive to compare experience as a whole before and after its establishment. The accompanying chart plots on a logarithmic scale annual averages of the stock of money from 1867 to 1958, as estimated by Anna J. Schwartz and myself in connection with our study for the National Bureau of Economic Research. It just so happens that the year 1914, when the Federal Reserve System began operation, divides this period nearly in two. A glance at the chart makes it clear that the forty-four years since 1914 have been characterized by considerably more instability in the stock of money than the forty-seven years before that date: in numerical terms, the standard deviation of the year-to-year percentage changes in the stock of money is about one and one-half times as large for the second period as for the first.[11] Of course, this difference reflects partly the two world wars during the second period, which raise special problems. But even if the war and immediate postwar years are omitted and attention concentrated on the peacetime years from, say, 1920 through 1939, and 1947 through 1959, the result is the same: the stock of money was more unstable during the thirty-three peacetime years of Federal Reserve control than during the prior forty-seven years. In numerical terms, the standard deviation of the year-to-year changes is one and one-fifth times as large for the second period as for the first.[12]

What is true of the stock of money is true also of economic conditions in general. The thirty-three peacetime years after World War I were among the most economically unstable in our history. The instability is concentrated in the period between the wars. Those two decades encompass three severe contractions: 1920–21, 1929–33, and 1937–38. There is no other twenty-year period in American history containing three comparably severe contractions.

This crude comparison does not of course prove that the Federal Reserve System failed to contribute to monetary stability. Perhaps the problems that the System had to handle were more severe than those that impinged on the earlier monetary structure. Perhaps greater instability of the economic system due to other forces produced the greater degree of monetary instability rather than the connection running in any important way in the other direction. Perhaps these forces would have

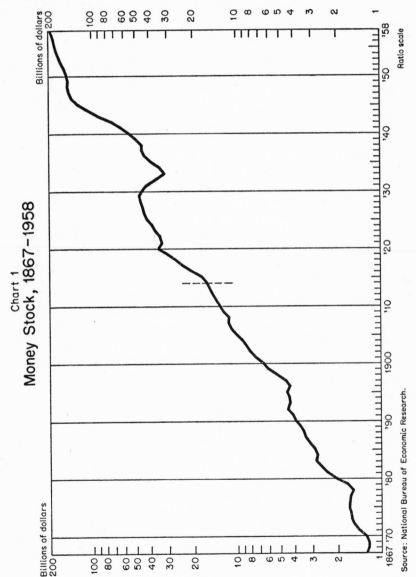

Chart 1
Money Stock, 1867–1958

Source: National Bureau of Economic Research.

produced an even greater degree of monetary instability under the earlier arrangements. In order to throw some light on these questions, let us examine some individual episodes.

The expansion of the money supply during the active phase of World War I requires little attention: until our entry into the war it was produced by the gold inflow from the belligerents to purchase war supplies, thereafter, by the use of the equivalent of the printing press to finance some war expenditures. Up to late 1918 or early 1919, the experience was the same as in earlier wars and the existence of the System made little difference to the general course of events. But then a difference emerges. In earlier wars, prices reached their peak at the end of the war, when government deficits were sharply reduced or eliminated. They would have again if the System had not been in existence. As it was, the mechanism developed to create money for government use continued to operate even after government deficits came to an end. Under Treasury pressure, the Reserve System maintained rediscount rates at their wartime level. From early 1919 to mid-1920 the money supply rose by over 20% and prices by nearly 25%. This postwar rise in money and prices would almost certainly not have occurred under the earlier system.

Toward the end of 1919, the Reserve System reversed its policy, raising discount rates at New York from 4 to 4¾% in November 1919, then to a uniform level of 6% at all Banks in late January or early February 1920—the sharpest single rise in the entire history of the System before or since—and again to 7% at New York in June 1920, some five months after the peak in business had been reached and one month after the price peak. It took some time for the effect of the change in policy to take hold, which explains why the System was induced to raise discount rates a third time even though the second rise had in fact probably been larger than was necessary. The System did not reverse its policy to any extent until May 1921, sixteen months after the cyclical peak and only two months before the cyclical trough, and then only mildly. The result was a collapse in prices by nearly 50%, one of the most rapid if not the most rapid on record, and a decline in the stock of money that is the sharpest in our record up to this date.

U.S. monetary policy clearly stands out as a major factor in this sharp rise and fall in prices and economic activity, not only in the United States but also internationally. To say this is not to criticize the monetary authorities, given their problem. The Federal Reserve System had been established in the expectation that the gold standard would continue to be the major determinant of the stock of money. No sooner had it been established than the war produced a large-scale abandonment of the gold standard. There was no strictly comparable American experience on which to base policy or to judge the effects of actions designed to stimulate or retard monetary expansion. In particular, there was no evidence on the length of the lag between action and effect. There was a natural if regrettable tendency to wait too long before stepping on the brake, as it were; then to brake too hard; then, when this did not bring monetary expansion to a halt very shortly, to brake yet again.

During the rest of the 1920's, both the stock of money and economic activity were relatively stable. These years produced widespread confidence, both inside and outside the System, that the new monetary arrangements were producing a high degree of stability and could continue to do so. In terms of these years this judgment was largely justified. Yet in retrospect, it is clear that problems were arising even then. The gold sterilization policy of the 1920's and the tight-money policy followed in the later 1920's to counter the stock market boom kept prices in this country stable or declining, and thereby increased the difficulty experienced by Britain in particular and other countries as well in maintaining the gold standard to which they had returned. All of the burden of adjustment of any potential balance of payments deficits was being imposed on them and the groundwork was thereby laid for the international financial difficulties of the early 1930's and Britain's 1931 departure from gold which had such important repercussions in the United States.

These U.S. policies were not of course the only factors rendering the maintenance of the gold standard by Britain difficult, and may not even be among the most important. Of the factors external to Britain, France's return to gold at a parity that turned out to undervalue the franc and thus attracted gold on a large scale was probably the most important.

The next important episode of instability was of course the 1929–33 contraction. Its early phase, from August 1929 to about October 1930, seemed very much in the mold of the usual cyclical contraction, though perhaps somewhat more severe, and rendered more dramatic by the stock market crash. During this period, the Federal Reserve described its policy as an "easy-money policy." In fact, even during these first fourteen months of the contraction, the stock of money fell by some 3%—a larger decline than during the whole of all but three preceding contractions, 1873–79, 1907–08, 1920–21, and all but one thereafter, that of 1937–38. And all the exceptions were unusually severe contractions by other indicators as well. The Federal Reserve was misled, as it has been so frequently before and since, by its tendency to look at the absolute level of the discount rate rather than at its relation to market rates or at the behavior of the money supply—a variant of the fallacy that would interpret a bond-support policy as a "neutral" policy. But in this initial phase, it is hard to trace any very direct effect of Federal Reserve policy on economic activity; the connection may as readily have been in the opposite direction.

The serious fault of the Federal Reserve dates from the end of 1930, when a series of bank failures, including the notable failure of the Bank of the United States in New York, changed the monetary character of the contraction. Prior to that date, there was no sign of a liquidity crisis—the ratio of currency to deposits was relatively stable or falling. From then on, the economy was plagued by recurrent liquidity crises. A wave of bank failures would taper down for a while, and then start up again as a few dramatic failures or other events produced a new loss of confidence in the banking system and a new series of runs on banks. As the public converted deposits into currency, the ratio of currency to deposits climbed, reaching a level in early 1933 more than two and a half times its level in late 1930.

This was precisely the kind of situation that had led to a banking panic under the earlier banking system and to a concerted suspension of the convertibility of deposits into currency. One of the major objectives of the Federal Reserve System was to prevent such a development. In the event it failed to do so. The panic and suspension of payments came anyway. But there was an important difference. Under the earlier system, the suspension of payments had been a therapeutic device that came early and served to prevent the liquidity crisis from producing any widespread failures of otherwise sound banks. This time, the suspension came after a large fraction of the banks had failed and after the economy had suffered three years of deflation. Moreover, when it came, it was incomparably more sweeping and severe than any earlier suspension.

There seems to me little doubt that the System could have prevented this monetary collapse—and indeed that it very likely would have done so if it had not been for accidents of personnel and the resulting shift of the center of power from New York to Washington. From the end of October 1930 through July 1931, nearly 1,400 banks holding $1 billion in deposits or about 2% of all deposits in commercial banks failed, the money stock declined by 6% in addition to the 3% decline up to October, and deposits in commercial banks fell by 8%. In face of this drastic liquidation of the commercial banking system, the books of the "lender of last resort" actually showed a slight decline in bills discounted and no change in total Federal Reserve credit outstanding, which stood at a level only half that at the end of 1928.

In the summer of 1931 there were many signs of recovery. But this incipient economic revival, if such it was, was nipped in the bud when, in August 1931, there was a renewed spurt of bank failures and when, in September, Britain went off the gold standard. The Federal Reserve reacted vigorously and promptly to the resultant external drain as it had not to the internal drain. After more than two years of severe economic contraction, the System raised discount rates sharply. For the New York Bank, the rate rose more sharply than it had within so brief a period in its whole history before or has since—from 1½% on October 8 to 2½% the next day and 3½% a week later. The measure arrested the gold drain, though ironically the French balances whose withdrawal the System most feared were withdrawn anyway the next spring. The measure was also accompanied by a spectacular increase in bank failures and runs on banks. All told, in the six months from August 1931 through January 1932, 1,860 banks with deposits of $1,449 million suspended operations, and total deposits in commercial banks fell by 15%.

A temporary reversal of policy in 1932 manifested in the purchase of $1 billion of government bonds slowed down the rate of decline. Had this measure been taken in 1931, it would almost surely have been sufficient to prevent the debacle just described. By 1932, it was too late to be more than a palliative and when the System ceased purchasing bonds and relapsed into passivity, the temporary improvement was followed by a renewed collapse terminating in the Banking Holiday of 1933. All told, from July 1929 to March 1933, the money stock fell by over a third, with over two-thirds of the decline coming after England's departure from the gold standard and the accompanying deflationary action by the System.

I have described this episode in some detail because it has played such an important role in forming—or should I say deforming—opinions about monetary policy. It was interpreted to mean that monetary policy is an ineffective instrument for stemming deflation. In fact it is a tragic testament to the harm that an inappropriate policy can do. It may well be that a different policy might not have prevented a severe contraction; it certainly could have made it much less severe than it was and could have prevented the collapse of the banking system. It is noteworthy that every country that followed Britain in going off gold experienced revival in 1931 or shortly thereafter; every country that followed the U.S. in accepting monetary deflation saw the contraction drag on to 1933 or later. It is exceedingly dubious that any comparable monetary collapse would have occurred under the pre-1914 banking system.

After 1933 the Federal Reserve System followed a policy of almost complete inactivity, both as a defense reaction to its failure to stem the contraction and because of the change in the intellectual climate of opinion which assigned priority to fiscal policy. The Reserve System's portfolio was kept almost perfectly constant, and the discount rate was hardly varied. In any event, since the discount rate was higher than short-term market rates, the discount mechanism was essentially inoperative. The Treasury conducted such active monetary policy as there was through its silver and gold purchase payments, through sterilization of gold in late 1936 and early 1937, and desterilization in late 1937 and early 1938—essentially open market operations—and through the Exchange Stabilization Fund. The one action that the Federal Reserve System took was to use newly granted powers to double reserve requirements in three steps in 1936 and 1937. The System did not intend these changes to have any immediate effect and did not believe they would; they were intended as a precautionary measure to absorb excess reserves. In fact, they had a severe deflationary impact. The first rise coincides with a slowing down of the rate of rise of the money supply; the second and third with the beginning of an absolute decline. The exceedingly severe contraction of 1937–38 might have occurred when it did anyway and it may well be that it derived more from an independent collapse in investment in reaction to other governmental policies than from the monetary action, but it hardly would have been as severe as it was in the absence of the deflationary pressure arising from the doubling of reserve requirements.

The most important monetary event after 1933 was the establishment of federal insurance of bank deposits. For reasons that we shall have occasion to consider in more detail in the next chapter, this measure renders banking panics all but impossible, an objective that the Reserve System had failed to achieve. It does so not by providing a source of liquidity to banks once "runs" begin, but by eliminating any reason for runs to begin. In my view, it has been the most important structural change in our monetary system in the direction of greater stability since the post-Civil War tax on state bank notes.

World War II was like earlier wartime episodes in its monetary aspects—the equivalent of the printing press was again used as a means of financing some wartime expenditures. As in World War I, postwar experience is more interesting for our purposes than the period of active war. This time, the price rise and the expansion of the stock of money continued for some thirty-six months rather than eighteen months beyond the end of the active fighting and for over two years rather than one year beyond the end of government deficits. This time the vehicle was not a relatively fixed discount rate but a relatively fixed pattern of yields on government securities. The maintenance of the fixed pattern, like the earlier maintenance of the fixed discount rate, meant the renunciation by the Reserve System of any power to control the stock of money—the stock of money had to be whatever was required to maintain the fixed pattern and was thus determined entirely by the actual and potential holders of government securities.

Fortunately, from 1946 until the outbreak of the Korean War, the fixed pattern did not involve any substantial inflationary pressure. The sharp rise in the price index in 1946 after the suspension of price control must be regarded more as a public unveiling of hitherto suppressed price rises than as a rise in prices properly measured. The money supply rose only mildly from 1946 to 1948 and so did prices, if allowance is made for the jump in the index just referred to. Both the money supply and prices fell slightly from 1948 to 1949 in the course of the economic recession. It is by no means clear why the relatively low absolute level of yields supported by the Federal Reserve was at first hardly below and then somewhat above the market yields consistent with price stability. The most plausible explanation is a widespread expectation of a major postwar price decline founded on the experience after World War I and strongly reinforced by the 1930's, which made the public at large willing to hold an unusually large volume of money and of low-yielding government securities relative to its income.

The failure of the 1948–49 recession to develop into a major contraction combined with the outbreak of the Korean War to produce a major change in expectations. A level of security yields that had been consistent with little change in the stock of money and in prices was associated with a rapid rise in both after mid-1950. This sharp price rise was not produced in any great measure by the printing of money to finance government expenditures, as in earlier wartime periods, but by the Federal Reserve's commitment to create whatever quantity of money was required to keep prices of government securities from declining below pre-designated levels. The obvious impotence of the Federal Reserve to do anything about this inflationary surge which its own policy was fostering was a clear case of governmental monetary actions serving as a highly destabilizing factor in the economy. It stimulated conflict between the Federal Reserve and the Treasury, not at first about the policy of supporting government securities but about the level of support. This conflict ultimately led to the Accord of 1951 and, some two years later, to the explicit abandonment of support.

Except for the sharp price rise in 1950–51, our monetary experience since 1948 or so has been admirable by previous standards. The year-to-year changes in the money supply have been relatively stable and so has economic activity. We have experienced three minor recessions in 1948–49, 1953–54, and 1957–58, but no major contractions and no substantial price rises other than the 1950–51 rise. This period is roughly comparable to earlier periods of relative stability—the 1880's, the decade or so before World War I, the 1920's. I am inclined myself to believe that the stability, or at least the avoidance of sharp declines, in the stock of money partly reflects an increased awareness on the part of the Federal Reserve System of the importance of a steady growth in the stock of money and partly represents a basic institutional change—the effect of federal deposit insurance in rendering highly unlikely a banking collapse—but it is too early yet to be certain that this is the case.

CONCLUSION

This sketch of our monetary experience has concentrated on the major economic fluctuations—those substantial inflations and severe contractions that have from time to time produced widespread distress and threatened our social cohesion. In respect of these, the record seems clear. Every such episode has been accompanied by a significant monetary disturbance. There has been no significant monetary disturbance not accompanied by a severe economic fluctuation. The monetary disturbances have had a largely independent origin in enough cases to establish a strong presumption that they are contributory causes rather than simply incidental effects of the economic fluctuations; that, while influences ran both ways, there was nothing in the nature of the economic fluctuation that made the monetary disturbances inevitable. This is clearly the case with the Bank War in the 1830's; the pressure for resumption in the 1870's; the silver agitation in the 1890's; the inflation and sharp contraction after World War I; the banking collapse of 1931 to 1933; and the bond support program after World War II. Finally, almost all the monetary disturbances have arisen either from inadequacies of governmental monetary policies or from controversy about them. Governmental intervention in monetary matters, far from providing the stable monetary framework for a free market that is its ultimate justification, has proved a potent source of instability.

In addition to these major economic fluctuations our economy has experienced recurrent fluctuations of a milder character, such as the three post-World War II business fluctuations. These milder fluctuations have been with us for at least two centuries and doubtless will be for a long time to come. They may well be an inevitable accompaniment of a private-market economy or indeed, in one form or other, of any dynamic society. It may be also that they are only less virulent members of the same species as the major fluctuations. Whether this is so or not, they clearly raise a very different problem for monetary policy. We know much more about how to prevent the major fluctuations from occurring than about how to render the minor fluctuations still milder, and it is much more urgent to do so.

If my reading of the historical record is in any large measure valid, it has important implications for the formulation of appropriate monetary arrangements. It means that the central problem is not to construct a highly sensitive instrument that can continuously offset instability introduced by other factors, but rather to prevent monetary arrangements from themselves becoming a primary source of instability. What we need is not a skilled monetary driver of the economic vehicle continuously turning the steering wheel to adjust to the unexpected irregularities of the route, but some means of keeping the monetary passenger who is in the back seat as ballast from occasionally leaning over and giving the steering wheel a jerk that threatens to send the car off the road. The chapters that follow try to outline such a monetary policy.

Chapter Two

The Tools of the Federal Reserve System

POWER OVER MONEY AND CREDIT is dispersed among a considerable number of governmental agencies: the Federal Reserve System; the Treasury, through its debt management operations, its Exchange Stabilization Fund, and its management of the trust funds; the Federal Deposit Insurance Corporation; the Federal Farm Banks; the various agencies concerned with housing credit, such as the Housing and Home Finance Agency, the Veterans Administration, the Federal National Mortgage Association; and so on in typical governmental confusion and profusion. The Federal Reserve System and the Treasury are however the two most active agencies and for simplicity I shall limit my discussion to them. In this chapter, I shall consider the tools of policy available to the Federal Reserve System; in the next, the related problem of debt management. The coordination of Reserve and Treasury policy with the policies of the other agencies, though important, lies outside our primary interests and I shall leave it there.

The financial powers of the Federal Reserve System can be classified into three related and overlapping categories.

First, there are the powers that enable the System to determine the total amount of money in existence or to alter the amount—these we may call the tools of monetary policy. The most important of them are rediscounting and the rediscount rate; power to change reserve requirements; and power to purchase and sell securities on the open market.

A second category of powers enables the System to affect the allocation of loans or of deposits or the structure of interest rates—these we may call the tools of specific credit policy. They include the definition of eligibility for rediscount, originally of the greatest importance but currently of minor significance; control over specific uses of credit, currently limited to margin requirements on security credit but at one time or another applied to consumer installment credit and real estate credit; and control over rates that member banks may pay on demand deposits and time deposits. The tools of monetary policy also enter into specific credit policy by affecting the competitive position of banks and the relative desirability of different assets to banks and other financial institutions and so altering the structure of interest rates. However, these effects are mostly secondary.

A third category of powers enables the System to supervise or regulate the operations of member banks. These include the power to discount or refuse to discount for individual member banks, the enforcement of legal limitations on the asset and liability structure of member banks, and the associated examination of the books of member banks.

In addition, of course, the System has powers that enable it to perform such service functions as check clearing, exchange of currency, and its fiscal duties for the Treasury.

This haphazard assortment of tools reflects mainly historical accident. Tools have been added from time to time; none have been subtracted except for the lapsing of temporary power to control consumer and real estate credit. The resulting collection is poorly adapted to the task of controlling the money supply, and renders that task more difficult. The aim of this chapter is to suggest how the collection of tools available to the Reserve System might best be streamlined. Such streamlining seems desirable almost whatever may be the criteria determining the changes in the stock of money that it is desired to produce. Hence the reforms suggested do not depend for their validity on any prior commitment in this respect. They are mostly of the nature of technical reforms.

The supervisory and regulatory powers of the Federal Reserve are relatively minor; this task is handled mostly by other agencies—the Federal Deposit Insurance Corporation, the Comptroller of the Currency, and the various state bodies charged with the regulation of banks. I shall accordingly pass over these powers, leaving any comment on them to the discussion of banking reform in the next chapter. Similarly, I shall neglect the service functions of the System.

TOOLS OF SPECIFIC CREDIT POLICY

The tools of specific credit policy—eligibility requirements, margin requirements, control over consumer and real estate credit, and control over interest paid by member banks on deposits—are more important, but I shall deal with them rather summarily in order to reserve most of the discussion for the tools of monetary policy. The first three are concerned with the specific use made of credit, and their enactment presumably reflected the belief that the market apportions credit improperly. The fourth, though it has similar effects, had a different origin, the belief that it would improve banking practices.

ELIGIBILITY REQUIREMENTS

Eligibility requirements date from the origin of the Federal Reserve System, which was set up by men mostly wedded to that ubiquitous fallacy, the real bills doctrine.[1] They viewed rediscounting as the major power of the Reserve System and thought that it could be made to produce the appropriate degree of "elasticity" in the money supply if it were restricted to the rediscounting of real bills, that is, loans made to finance bona fide self-liquidating commercial transactions. The eligibility requirements were imposed to achieve this objective. Although the words remained the same, the substance of the eligibility requirements was changed radically by the World War I extension of discounting to loans backed by government securities, loans that could hardly qualify as "real bills" under the earlier doctrine. The requirements were further attenuated in the Glass-Steagall Act of 1932 and the Banking Act of 1935, in response to Federal Reserve claims, which in my view had little justification, that eligibility limitations had been an important factor accounting for the failure of the System to prevent the prior banking collapse. Currently they have little except historical significance. So far as policy is concerned, the System has long recognized that the kind of collateral on which it extends credit has essentially no connection with the ultimate use made of the credit. Hence, even if controlling the use of credit were desirable, which I believe it is not, eligibility requirements would be a poor device for doing so.

CONTROL OVER MARGIN REQUIREMENTS

Control over margin requirements was a consequence of the ill-fated attempt by the Reserve System in 1928 and 1929 to prevent "credit" from being used in the stock market boom. The Reserve System resorted to "moral suasion" or "direct pressure" as it was then called—its usual recourse when for one reason or another it is unwilling to use its other powers. It found again, as it had fully recognized at an earlier date and as it was to find again when similar techniques were invoked during the Korean episode, that the only effect was to change the form, not the substance, of the credit transactions. Accordingly, it sought additional powers. When the Banking Acts of 1933 and 1935 revised Federal Reserve powers, an attempt was made to restrict the use of credit for "speculative" purposes and the Securities Exchange Act of 1934 granted the System power to impose margin requirements on security loans.

In 1928 and 1929, the System's concern with the stock market led it to follow a general credit policy that was too tight for general business and too easy to stop the stock market boom. The stock market boom doubtless had other effects on the subsequent course of events, but I suspect that this effect on Reserve policy may well have been the most damaging. Because of their dramatic quality, movements in stock prices command more attention from the System and others than their role as a source rather than a reflection of economic changes justifies. Assignment to the System of specific responsibility for the use of credit in the stock market reinforces this tendency. So long as the System has its present range of discretion about policy, it should keep its eye fixed on general economic conditions and not be diverted by what happens in particular sectors except as indicators of general conditions. Personally, I see no justification for singling out credit extended to purchase or hold securities for special attention. But if this is to be done, it should be as part of a policy directed at regulation of security markets and by an agency charged with special responsibility for such markets, not by the Federal Reserve System.

CONTROL OVER CONSUMER INSTALLMENT CREDIT

Control over consumer installment credit, now happily lapsed, was introduced first by executive order in September 1941, abolished by Congress in November 1947, granted again for nine months in the summer of 1948, again after the outbreak of the Korean War, and repealed in 1952. Control over real estate credit was in effect for only the last of these periods—from October 1950 to May 1952. The wartime introduction of consumer credit control, part of the general wartime reliance on direct controls, was rendered largely irrelevant by the suppression of the production of many durable consumer goods shortly thereafter. It was reintroduced and real estate controls added later mostly because the bond support program immobilized the chief weapons available to the System to counter inflationary pressures, and it was thought or perhaps only hoped that these direct controls might be a substitute.

CONTROL OVER INTEREST PAID BY BANKS ON DEPOSITS

Provisions prohibiting the payment of interest by member banks on demand deposits and giving the Federal Reserve power to fix the rate of interest on time deposits were enacted after the banking collapse of the early 1930's. They were justified on the grounds that the payment of interest on deposits had led banks to follow a riskier investment policy in order to increase earnings than they otherwise would have done and had thus contributed to the banking collapse. This argument for the restriction of interest payments on deposits has a long history; it was made for example by O. M. W. Sprague in his book on *Crises under the National Banking Act* issued by the National Monetary Commission in 1910. However, fallacies no less than truths can be ancient. The limitation of interest rates is a clear case of governmental price fixing. The argument for it is a usual cartel argument for price fixing—that price fixing is in the public interest because the members of the cartel will be led to engage in unethical or socially unwise activities unless they receive "respectable" or "reasonable" profits. In fact, of course, fixing the price that a bank pays its depositors does not affect in any way its incentive to distribute its assets in the most profitable fashion. If the prohibition were effective, if it initially increased returns to existing banks, and if entry into banking were free, the effect would be to attract additional resources into banking until returns to skill and capital invested in banking were again at roughly competitive levels. If the other conditions were satisfied but entry were restricted, which in part it is through the necessity to obtain a franchise, the effect would be a higher market value of bank stock, and roughly the competitive return to skill and per dollar of market value of capital. How the capital gains to the initial owners would lead subsequent owners to sacrifice potential profits to an allegedly socially beneficial avoidance of risk is something of a mystery—even if it be granted, as I do not, both that such action would be socially desirable and that the willingness of individuals to sacrifice private interest to an assumed social interest is really correlated with income and wealth.

In practice, the prohibition of the payment of interest on demand deposits has been largely ineffective. It was imposed at a time when interest rates were so low that banks were led to impose service charges and, prohibition or no prohibition, would have paid little or no interest. For most of the time since, there has been ample scope for competition in services rendered and charges for them. Until recently, much the same has been true about the limitation of the rate that may be paid on time deposits.

These limitations were initially welcomed by commercial banks precisely because they involved governmental enforcement of a maximum price on a cost item in the banking business, and thus a governmentally enforced monopsony or buying cartel. More recently, however, as competition has developed for time deposits from other financial intermediaries such as building and loan associations, mutual savings banks and the like, the banks have been restive about the limit imposed on time deposit rates—a course of events that is not untypical for buying and selling cartels in general. In all of the extensive discussions about the alleged competitive disadvantages imposed on commercial banks relative to other financial intermediaries by use of the banks as a vehicle for monetary policy, this is one of the few valid points that have been made—being subject to price fixing has become a competitive disadvantage that serves no discernible monetary purpose.

These tools of specific credit policy are the kinds of powers that I had in mind in the first chapter when I referred to the danger that government intervention would spread from areas where it is appropriate to areas where it is inappropriate. Each is a specific control that affects particular lines of activity, involves detailed intervention into economic affairs, and has little connection with the essential functions of governmental monetary authorities, which consist in setting an external limit on the quantity of money and preventing the economic equivalent of counterfeiting. Except for eligibility requirements, all date from the 1930's or later. Their enactment was part of the general shift of sentiment toward the approval of more extensive and more detailed government intervention in economic affairs. As this sentiment has ebbed, so has the enthusiasm for them. None is necessary in order for the Federal Reserve to control the total quantity of money and none has much, if any, effect on the quantity of money. Their effect, if any, is on the allocation of loanable funds among different uses and on the structure, rather than the level, of interest rates. Those that are still in effect should be abolished, or at the very least removed from the Reserve System; and no similar powers should be enacted.

To maintain perspective, I should perhaps add that the unfortunate effects of these controls are far overshadowed in quantitative importance by the corresponding effects of the various preferential credit schemes that have been enacted for such fields as housing, agriculture, and small business, which are outside the self-imposed scope of this book.

TOOLS OF MONETARY POLICY

I turn now to the major powers of the Reserve System, the tools of monetary policy—open market operations, rediscounting, and variable reserve requirements. With respect to these, I shall argue that open market operations alone are a sufficient and efficient tool for monetary policy. Rediscounting is an anachronistic survival of an earlier day and an earlier need. Its original function has disappeared. Variation in reserve requirements, though a more recent innovation, shares with rediscounting the property of being a technically poor instrument for controlling the stock of money. Both should be eliminated or greatly altered. In presenting this view, I shall first demonstrate that open market operations are a sufficient tool and then examine rediscounting and variable reserve requirements.

THE SUFFICIENCY OF OPEN MARKET OPERATIONS

The total stock of money in existence at any time, by which I shall mean currency plus commercial bank deposits adjusted to exclude interbank deposits, U.S. government deposits, and items in process of collection, can be expressed as a function of three variables: (1) the amount of currency outside the Treasury and the Federal Reserve available for use by the public and as vault cash plus bank deposits with Federal Reserve Banks—the amount of high-powered money, as it is generally termed; (2) the ratio of the public's currency holdings to its deposits, or the currency-deposit ratio; and (3) the ratio of commercial banks' holdings of high-powered money (including both vault cash and deposits with Reserve Banks) to their deposit liabilities or the reserve-deposit ratio.[2] Given the value of the two ratios, the stock of money is directly proportional to the amount of high-powered money. Given the amount of high-powered money, the stock of money is higher, the lower the currency-deposit ratio, and also the lower the reserve-deposit ratio.

Currently, the Federal Reserve can affect the amount of high-powered money in two ways: by buying or selling securities and by altering discount rates and thereby giving member banks a greater or lesser incentive to rediscount with, or borrow from, the System. In addition, the amount of high-powered money is affected by factors outside the direct control of the System. The most important of these are changes in the amount of member-bank rediscounting or borrowing occurring for reasons other than alterations in the discount rate, changes in the amount of Federal Reserve "float" arising out of its check-clearing operations, gold flows, and changes in Treasury balances in cash or at Reserve Banks.

The Federal Reserve cannot currently affect the currency-deposit ratio directly. Its actions may have indirect effects, for example, by altering interest rates or the level of prices which in their turn may influence the currency-deposit ratio that the public seeks to maintain. A historical example of a rather different kind of indirect effort occurred in the early 1930's when the failure of the Federal Reserve to expand the amount of high-powered money sufficiently to prevent widespread bank failures arising out of initial attempts by the public to convert deposits into currency helped to intensify the loss of confidence in banks. In the main, however, the Reserve System must regard the currency-deposit ratio as determined by forces outside its control which shape the preferences of the public about the form in which it wants to hold its cash balances.

The Federal Reserve System can currently affect the reserve-deposit ratio by altering reserve requirements and thereby the amount of high-powered money that banks seek to hold relative to their deposits, although there is, of course, no fixed mechanical relation between reserve requirements and the actual reserve-deposit ratio. In addition, the reserve-deposit ratio may change for a variety of other reasons, such as shifts in deposits between demand and time accounts and among banks which hold different ratios of high-powered money to deposits, or changes in the rates of interest banks can earn on assets or must pay to borrow or in anticipated demands for conversion of deposits, which alter the amount of high-powered money banks wish to hold.

To demonstrate that open market operations alone would be sufficient for the conduct of monetary policy, almost regardless of the objectives toward which that policy is directed, let us assume for the moment that the Reserve System cannot make loans to its member banks or discount paper for them and that reserve requirements are frozen at their present level, with the Reserve System having no power to raise or lower them. In all other respects, we may suppose the Reserve System to operate just as it does now, and its deposit liabilities to remain the only medium of exchange satisfying the reserve requirements of member banks.[3] Member banks would meet any needs for additional reserve funds by borrowing from other banks, through the Federal Funds market or otherwise, or by disposing of assets, as they do mostly now and as they did almost exclusively for a long period in the 1930's.

Under these hypothetical arrangements, the Reserve System could influence the stock of money only by changing the amount of high-powered money, and it could change the amount of high-powered money only by buying and selling securities.[4] But these techniques would not only be adequate to produce any changes deemed desirable, they would in fact enable such changes to be made through open market operations more smoothly than at present and with less slippage between the desired change and the actual change.

Let us suppose, for example, that it were desired to expand the stock of money at a specified rate. The Federal Reserve would then purchase securities in order to increase the volume of high-powered money. The amount it purchased would depend on two factors: first, the amount by which it wanted to increase high-powered money; second, its estimate of likely changes in other factors affecting high-powered money.

To determine the first would, as now, require allowance for possible changes in the currency-deposit and the reserve-deposit ratios, that is, it would require an estimate of the rate at which high-powered money would have to increase to produce the desired rate of increase in the stock of money. With respect to this step, the one difference between the hypothetical and the present arrangements is in the factors affecting the reserve-deposit ratio. At present, this ratio is affected by the availability of rediscount facilities and the possibility that reserve requirements may be changed. The significance of these factors varies considerably over time and hence they render the reserve-deposit ratio more unstable than it would be in their absence. In consequence, it would be possible to estimate the change in high-powered money required to produce the desired change in the stock of money somewhat more accurately than now. However the difference in this respect would not be large.

A more important difference is in the second step, the likely changes in other factors affecting high-powered money. Currently, these other factors include the amount of member bank borrowing at the Federal Reserve. This sum is not only variable for other reasons but, more important, is affected in a highly variable fashion by Federal Reserve open market purchases. Member banks are likely to use some part of the increased high-powered money they obtain as a result of such purchases to pay off indebtedness at the Reserve System. If the part they used were fixed, it would simply mean that a dollar of Federal Reserve purchases would add, not a dollar to high-powered money, but a stable fraction of a dollar, say 80 cents, so that the System would have to buy a dollar and a quarter's worth of securities to increase high-powered money by a dollar. In fact, the part used is not fixed but varies widely depending on a host of circumstances affecting both the amount of member bank borrowing outstanding and the desire of member banks to increase or reduce borrowing. Under the hypothetical arrangements, member bank borrowing would be non-existent and a dollar of Reserve purchases would add a dollar to high-powered money. Though allowance would still have to be made for other factors such as gold flows and changes in Treasury balances, the problem of doing so would be no different than at present. Hence, there would be a decidedly closer and more predictable relation between Reserve System purchases and changes in high-powered money under the hypothetical arrangements than at present.

The same conclusions are valid if it is desired to reduce rather than increase the stock of money at a specified rate. The System would then sell securities to reduce the volume of high-powered money. Again, the amount by which it would want to reduce high-powered money would depend on the anticipated behavior of the currency-deposit and reserve-deposit ratios, and the second ratio could be estimated somewhat more accurately under the hypothetical than under the present arrangements. The amount of securities it would have to sell to achieve the desired reduction in high-powered money would again depend on the anticipated behavior of other factors affecting high-powered money and again, one of the most variable of these, member bank borrowing, would be absent under the hypothetical arrangements, so that it would be possible to estimate more accurately the amount that needed to be sold.

The greater ease in producing desired changes in the stock of money also implies that it would be easier to avoid undesired changes, and this for the same reasons. Some existing sources of such changes would be eliminated under the hypothetical arrangements and no new ones introduced.

The limit to the expansion in the stock of money that could be produced by open market operations alone is set by the amount of securities available for the System to buy—though its gold reserve requirements might as now set a narrower limit; the limit to the contraction in the stock of money, by the amount of securities available for the System to sell. At present, these limits are so wide as to be largely irrelevant: Federal Reserve purchase of all outstanding marketable U.S. government securities would involve something like a quadrupling of the stock of money under the hypothetical arrangements; Federal Reserve sale of all securities in its portfolio, more than a halving of the stock of money. Within these limits, the System could produce any change in the stock of money it wished through open-market operations alone. The only time, historically, when these limits clearly hampered Federal Reserve operations was shortly after its establishment. Large inflows of gold after the outbreak of the European War in 1914 added to the stock of high-powered money and the Reserve System was powerless to offset this inflow because it had no earning assets to sell. The Reserve System regarded itself as hampered also in 1935–37, when excess reserves were larger than the System's security holdings, an episode to which I shall return. As a practical matter, such situations are not likely to arise again. In principle, however, it would be desirable to give the Reserve System power to issue its own securities, as has frequently been proposed, in order to assure that such situations could not arise.

I have expressed this analysis in terms of changes in the stock of money because, for reasons that I trust will become clear in the course of this book, the stock of money seems to me the desirable variable in terms of which to express Federal Reserve policy, whatever may be the particular pattern of change in the stock of money that it is desired to produce. However, the conclusions do not depend on this proposition. Let us suppose policy were expressed in some other terms—say, to take the alternative that would perhaps command widest support, "the" interest rate, to which we may give operational content by interpreting it to mean a weighted average of market interest rates on a specified list of securities. Under the hypothetical arrangements, the System can affect this average rate directly by buying or selling the securities in question, if they are of a kind it is authorized to buy and sell, and, indirectly, by altering the high-powered money in the hands of the public and thereby the willingness of banks and the non-bank public to purchase the securities in question. If the desired change in the interest rate can be achieved under present arrangements, then it can also be achieved under the hypothetical arrangements, subject only to the limitation that it not require changes in high-powered money greater than the available stock of securities the Reserve System can buy or sell, a limit of no practical significance. It is rather more difficult to establish that open market operations would be a more effective tool for this purpose in the absence of rediscounting and variable reserve requirements than it is now. The reason for this is that we know too little about the connection between changes in particular interest rates and in the money supply to be at all specific. But since persons who favor the use of interest rate changes as a guide or criterion for monetary policy generally regard changes in the stock of money as a major channel through which interest rates are affected, a more stable and predictable relation between open market operations and resultant changes in the money supply would presumably also imply a more stable and predictable relation between open market operations and changes in particular interest rates.

The sufficiency of open market operations as a tool for monetary policy is not, of course, a decisive reason for relying on this tool alone. Under some circumstances, discounting alone or variable reserve requirements alone might be sufficient; and under these or other circumstances, these other tools might achieve other desirable objectives that would justify rendering open market operations less effective. Let us therefore examine these other tools.

REDISCOUNTING

As noted in the first chapter, the Federal Reserve System was created by men whose outlook on the goals of central banking was shaped by the money panics during the national banking era. The main problem requiring solution seemed to them to be banking crises produced by, or resulting in, a widespread desire on the part of the public to shift from deposits to currency, generally because of a loss of confidence in banks arising out of a few notable bank or commercial failures. Under a fractional reserve banking system, widespread conversion of deposits into currency requires either an increase in high-powered money or a drastic shrinkage in the total amount of money. Prior to the Federal

Reserve System, a sizable increase in high-powered money generally could come only from gold imports. This took time and required a fairly drastic incentive. In consequence, a serious liquidity crisis could seldom be met in this way in the first instance. An individual bank might be able to convert its assets into currency; the system as a whole could not do so. The attempt by many individual banks to do so produced pressure for wholesale liquidation that led to contraction of the total money supply. Unless the process were halted fairly early, the attempted liquidation would drive down the prices of bank assets and render most banks technically insolvent.

As already noted, the therapeutic device that developed was the so-called suspension of payments—an agreement among banks, generally through their clearing house associations, that they would honor all requests to transfer deposits "through the clearing house," but would refuse to convert deposits into currency on demand, though continuing to do so for some purposes and for some customers. The suspension of payments in this sense did not involve even the temporary closing of the banks on any large scale or the cessation of their financial operations—as occurred during the much more drastic Banking Holiday of 1933. It meant rather the creation of two only partly convertible media of payments, currency and deposits, with deposits only imperfectly convertible into currency and hence with currency at a premium in terms of deposits. Once adjustment was made to the use of two such media of payments convertible into one another at a flexible rather than a fixed rate, the suspension could continue for months on end, as it did at times, without producing an economic breakdown and indeed in conjunction with economic revival.

The solution to the problem of panics embodied in the Federal Reserve Act was, in the words of its title, "to provide an elastic currency." Federal Reserve money was designed to differ from other forms of money by being subject to substantial change in quantity over short periods of time for reasons other than the immediate profitability of either the issuer or, as with specie, the importer or exporter. In this way, when depositors wished to convert deposits into currency, additional high-powered money could be made available in the form of Federal Reserve notes. Fundamentally, "elasticity" was aimed at not in the total amount of money but in the amount of one kind of money—currency—relative to another—deposits—though there was of course much confusion then as now between these two kinds of elasticity. Rediscounting was designed as the means whereby additional high-powered money could be put into circulation and subsequently retired. By rediscounting their assets, banks could convert them into the currency which their customers were demanding without reducing the reserves of other banks. The Reserve System was to be a "lender of last resort," ready to provide liquidity in a time of crisis to satisfy a widespread demand for currency that otherwise would produce either suspension of payments or a substantial decline in the total stock of money.

Rediscounting was therefore not originally intended to be used continuously to determine or alter the total stock of money. When the Act became law, the gold standard ruled supreme. It was taken for granted that it would continue to do so and that it would dominate the longer-term movements in the total stock of money. This view is reflected in the gold reserve ratios that were incorporated in the Federal Reserve Act. During and after World War I, the gold standard changed its character and the gold reserve ratio became a largely irrevelant guide for short-term movements. Rediscounting then developed into one of the two blades of the scissors continuously controlling the stock of money, open market operations being the other. In the 1929–33 contraction, the kind of situation developed that had been contemplated when the System was established and that an elastic currency issued through rediscounting had been designed to handle. In the event, these tools did not enable the System to cope with the crisis. Whether they need have been inadequate if differently managed is a moot question.

One result of the banking collapse was the enactment of federal insurance of bank deposits. Its purpose was to protect depositors against the kind of cruel losses they had experienced during the preceding years, not primarily to solve the problem of bank panics. It has, however, succeeded in doing so where rediscounting failed. Although deposits are technically insured only up to $10,000, bank failures involving losses to depositors have become almost a thing of the past. Banks still become insolvent, but they no longer fail. Instead, they tend to be merged with other banks or to be reorganized, with the Federal Deposit Insurance Corporation assuming responsibility for the bad assets. An indirect result has been to prevent any chain reaction such as used to occur. Even if a bank fails or is reorganized, there is no reason for depositors in other banks to become concerned. Changes in the ratio of deposits to currency still occur as a result of changed preferences. Such changes, however, even if sizable, tend to be gradual and do not involve runs on individual banks. A liquidity crisis involving such runs on a widespread scale is now almost inconceivable. The need for rediscounting in order for the Reserve System to serve as "a lender of last resort" has therefore become obsolete, not because the function has been taken over by someone else but because it no longer needs to be performed. To avoid misunderstanding, I should perhaps add that while federal deposit insurance has performed a signal service in rendering the banking system panic-proof, it does not seem to me the most desirable method of achieving this end and I shall suggest an alternative in the next chapter.

Having lost its initial function, rediscounting has acquired three very different and less critical roles. In the first place, it is a means whereby member banks can obtain funds from time to time at a lower cost than by alternative devices. In this respect, it involves special governmental assistance to a particular group of financial institutions. It is hard to see why it is appropriate or necessary for government to render such assistance or why commercial banks should be singled out to receive it. The capital market is a well-functioning and sensitive market, and banks can readily manage to provide for special needs in other ways—as for example they did throughout the later 1930's when, for reasons I shall mention shortly, rediscounting was hardly resorted to.

In the second place, rediscounting is a means whereby member banks can readily adjust their reserve balances to conform to reserve requirements when they unexpectedly discover that they are likely to be in deficit. Other means are however available and widely used for this purpose, the most notable among them in recent years being the Federal Funds market. In consequence this function, like the preceding, is solely a convenience offered to member banks.

In the third place, as already noted, rediscounting is a means whereby the Reserve System can influence the total amount of high-powered money in existence and thereby the total stock of money. This is its major current function and the function in terms of which it must basically be judged. And it so happens that rediscounting is a technically defective tool for this purpose.

The distinctive feature of rediscounting is that the initiative to rediscount is in the hands of the member banks. In consequence, the Reserve System cannot itself determine the amount of money it creates through the discount window or, for that matter, by a combination of the discount window and the open market. It can affect the amount of discounting by exercising discretion with respect to the banks for whom it will discount and the amount of discounting it will do for individual banks, or by changing the discount rate and thus the incentive on the part of banks to discount. The exercise of discretion is an undesirable kind of specific credit control that involves detailed intervention into the affairs of individual banks and arbitrary decisions by governmental officials. Moreover, it is incapable of being applied in a sufficiently sensitive way to produce predictable results over short periods. Hence, it is not even an efficient tool for controlling the amount of rediscounting. Most of the time, it has been held in abeyance. It has been brought into play generally only when the System has wished to avoid using its major weapons of discount rates or open market operations; notably in 1919, when the rediscount rate was being kept unchanged under Treasury pressure; in 1928 and 1929, in connection with the use of direct pressure to discourage so-called speculative loans; and in 1950–51, when the bond-support program was in effect. Whatever else is done about rediscounting, this feature should be changed. If rediscounting is retained, it should be a right, not a privilege, freely available to all member banks on specified terms.

The discount rate is the primary means used to influence the amount of discounting, so much so that "discount policy" is generally regarded as concerned exclusively with setting the discount rate. In practice, the discount rate has been used as a discontinuous instrument, changes being made only at substantial intervals and by sizable amounts. This operation by fits and starts introduces unnecessary instability into the economy. It also means that changes in the discount rate are newsworthy and attract attention. There is speculation about what they will be and much significance is read into them when they occur. If the System could predict accurately the future course of events and could establish an unambiguous connection between changes in the discount rate and its predictions, these "announcement effects" might be highly desirable, since individuals would then be led to behave in a way that would reinforce the System's actions—though in that case, the same result could almost surely be attained simply by publishing the System's predictions. As it is, the "announcement effects" are an additional source of uncertainty in the economy.

A second defect of the discount rate is the extreme difficulty of predicting the effect of a change in the rate on the amount of discounting, let alone on the stock of money. The effect on the willingness of member banks to borrow is very different under different circumstances, depending on such factors as the level of other rates of interest, the state of the demand for loans and the supply of funds from other sources, the investment opportunities available, and so on.

A closely related defect is, in my view, much the most important. The discount rate is something that the Federal Reserve System must continually change in order to keep the effect of its monetary policy unchanged. But changes in the rate are interpreted as if they meant changes in policy. Consequently both the System and outsiders are led to misinterpret the System's actions and the System is led to follow policies different from those it intends to follow.

The key point underlying these perhaps cryptic statements is one that became familiar in the course of the discussion of the post-World War II bond support program: a constant absolute rate of interest, whether it be the yield on government securities or a discount rate, does not in any relevant sense mean a constant monetary policy. If market rates rise, while discount rates do not, the incentive to discount is increased. This will tend to produce an increase in the amount of credit extended through discounting, an increase in the total amount of Federal Reserve credit outstanding, and a faster rate of growth of the stock of money than would otherwise have occurred. Conversely, if market rates fall, while discount rates do not, the incentive to discount is reduced, which will tend to reduce discounting and the amount of Federal Reserve credit outstanding, and to reduce the rate of growth of the stock of money. The same discount rate can thus correspond to "easy" money or "tight" money, however those ambiguous terms are defined, depending on the level of market rates; and maintaining the discount rate constant may imply a shift from "easy" money to "tight" money or conversely. In order to keep the degree of "ease" or "tightness" constant, the discount rate must be continuously changed.

Failure to recognize this point, and a tendency to regard the absolute level of the discount rate—or its level relative to some earlier date— as a measure of "tightness" or "ease" has been perhaps the single most pervasive source of confusion and error in the System's experience. In 1920, this fallacy was one reason why the System followed an unduly tight policy and maintained it too long. The discount rate of 6% imposed by all the Reserve Banks in January–February of 1920 and perhaps even the 7% imposed by the New York and three other Reserve Banks in June 1920 would probably not have been high enough to have prevented the money stock from rising if they had been imposed in 1919. By late 1920, these rates were forcing a drastic monetary contraction, yet they were maintained, becoming increasingly "tight" in their effects, until May 1921. The mild reduction at that time still meant a relatively "tight" policy.

From 1929 to 1933, the System kept repeating that it was following an "easy money" policy, pointing to the successive declines in discount rates—aside from the disastrous rise in the fall of 1931. Yet market rates were falling so much more rapidly that by any relevant test the System's policy must be adjudged exceedingly tight—certainly if either the behavior of the money supply or the condition of financial institutions is taken as the guide.

The System has been widely regarded as following a very "easy" money policy in the later 1930's. In fact, the discount rate, though low in an absolute sense by historical standards, exceeded market rates on short-term funds by a wider margin than at any previous time, with the exception only of a few months before the 1933 Banking Holiday, when the discount rate was even farther above short-term market rates. As a result, discounting fell into almost complete disuse in the later 1930's. The substantial and relatively rapid increase in the money stock from 1934 to 1936 and again from 1938 to 1940 owed nothing to easy money policy: it reflected entirely a large gold inflow. The gold inflow in its turn was produced at first mostly by the Treasury's gold and silver purchase programs reinforced by the flight of capital from Europe after Hitler's accession to power, then mostly by the flight of capital to the United States as the threat of war increased, reinforced by the gold and silver purchase programs.

The ill-fated bond support program of World War II and the postwar years is the most widely recognized example of the fallacy in question.

A more recent and more sophisticated version of the fallacy is the emphasis that was placed for a time on "free reserves" as a criterion of the "ease" or "tightness" of monetary policy, and to some extent still is. "Free reserves" are defined as the difference between the reserve balances of member banks and the sum of their required reserves and their borrowings from the System, or, equivalently, the difference between "excess reserves" and "borrowings." Arithmetically, it is clear that any given level of free reserves is consistent with either a rapid increase in the money supply or a rapid decrease. Both excess reserves and borrowings can remain constant, yet total and required reserves rise or fall at any rate, and excess reserves and borrowings can both change, yet their differences remain the same. Economically, there is presumably some level of free reserves that banks desire to maintain at any given time, a level that they try neither to increase by liquidating assets nor to decrease by acquiring assets. I shall call this level "desired free reserves." If the Reserve System tries to maintain a higher level by open market operations, the banks will seek to use the excess to add to their assets and in the process will increase the money supply and required reserves, and so reduce free reserves. The System can frustrate the banks by creating still more high-powered money, which will produce a continued increase in the money supply. Conversely, if the System tries to maintain a lower level of free reserves than desired, it can do so only by forcing a decline in the money stock. At any given time, therefore— and this is the element of validity in the free reserves doctrine—there is a level of free reserves consistent with no change in the money supply; higher levels imply an increase in the money supply and the higher the level, the more rapid the increase; and conversely for lower levels. But the levels corresponding to constant, increasing, or decreasing money supply do not remain the same over time. What matters is the size of free reserves relative to desired free reserves, not their absolute size. And the level of free reserves that banks desire is not itself a constant. It depends on the conditions of demand and supply for funds, on market rates of interest and their relation to the discount rate. Let the discount rate be unchanged, but market rates fall, and banks will desire to maintain larger free reserves. A level of free reserves that formerly was consistent with, let us say, a rate of rise in the stock of money of 3% a year, may now imply a rate of rise of 0%—this is the way in which the crude fallacy about discount rates enters in this more sophisticated analysis. I rather suspect that something like this is what happened in 1957 and accounts for the System being as tight as it was in the final months of that year.

As the 1957 example suggests, the fact that the same discount rate or the same level of free reserves implies different rates of monetary expansion, is particularly unfortunate at cyclical peaks. The System like the rest of us is unlikely to recognize that a decline is under way until some time after it has begun. In the meantime, the maintenance of the same discount rate or the same level of free reserves implies deflationary monetary pressure. In this way, there is an automatic tendency for a peak in business to produce a reduction in the rate of increase in the stock of money, just the opposite of the automatic reaction that most students would regard as desirable.

A final disadvantage of the use of the discount rate to control the amount of rediscounting is that it tends to promote confusion between what might be called the "monetary" effects of monetary policy—the effects on the stock of money—and the "credit" effects—the effects on recorded rates of interest and other conditions in the credit market. It is easy to see why these two should be confused. In modern financial systems, the creation of money is linked with lending and investing activity and changes in the stock of money generally take place through the credit markets. There is, however, no necessary connection. In an economy with a pure commodity money, for example, changes in the stock of money would take place through the purchase and sale of a commodity and not through credit markets at all. In practice, the actual link between the stock of money and credit conditions has varied widely. But the fact that there is a link has tended to lead to undue emphasis on the means whereby the money stock is changed rather than on the change itself. An ancient example of the confusion is the "real bills" fallacy already referred to. More recently, the change in economic ideas associated with the name of John Maynard Keynes led to an almost complete neglect of the "monetary" effects of monetary policy and concentration on the "credit" effects. Changes in the stock of money were treated as if they had no effect except insofar as they led to changes in a limited range of recorded market interest rates and thereby to changes in flows of spending. Analysis of the effects of monetary policy, both inside and outside the System, have therefore tended to be restricted to the level of recorded interest rates and movements in them to the complete neglect of changes in the quantity of money.[5]

It is analytically possible to treat all effects of changes in the quantity of money as taking place via changes in interest rates and their effects in turn on flows of spending. But to do so in a comprehensive way requires taking account of a much broader range of rates of interest than "recorded market" rates, for example, implicit rates entering into consumer decisions about stocks of durable goods to hold.

The confusion between the "monetary" and the "credit" effects of Reserve policy is an evil almost regardless of the views one may hold about the economic importance of changes in the stock of money or the channels through which such changes exert their influence. The Federal Reserve System occupies a commanding role under present circumstances in determining the stock of money—it can make the stock of money whatever it wants within very wide limits and to a high degree of precision. By contrast, it is one of many institutions in the capital market. It may be able to fix the yield on a few securities but only by sacrificing its control over the stock of money and even then only within fairly narrow limits. It cannot for long determine the whole structure of yields on capital assets. These propositions have surely been adequately demonstrated by postwar experience in this and other countries. Hence even if one were to believe—as I do not—that changes in the stock of money are relatively unimportant in their economic effect compared to changes in the capital market, and exert their influence predominantly by affecting recorded rates, the Reserve System's role is to control the stock of money. Its tools should be judged by their efficiency in enabling it to do so, though one might then wish to determine what changes it should make in the stock of money on the basis of the changes it was desired to produce in recorded interest rates. The fact that discounting means the setting of a specific interest rate fosters the belief that the System is directly controlling rates of interest and that its aim is to do so. This leads both the System and outsiders to misjudge its policy. It also inhibits Reserve policy because the Reserve System is attributed credit or blame for matters that are in fact outside of its control. It is described as aiming at a "higher" or "lower" level of interest rates when in practice any effects on interest rates may be entirely incidental to its purpose. It may, and I would say should, be raising or lowering discount rates not in order to affect interest rates but to affect the rate of change in the stock of money.

To avoid these disadvantages, rediscounting should be eliminated. The Federal Reserve would then no longer have to announce a discount rate or to change it; it would then have direct control over the amount of high-powered money it created; it would not be a source of instability alike by its occasional changes in the discount rate and by the unintended changes in the "tightness" or "ease" of policy associated with an unchanged rate, nor would it be misled by these unintended changes; and it would be less subject to being diverted from its main task by the attention devoted to the "credit" effects of its policy.

If rediscounting were eliminated, one minor function now performed by the discount rate would need to be provided for in some other way. Since required reserves are calculated after the event and need to be estimated in advance, some discrepancies between required and actual reserves are unavoidable, yet some penalty must be imposed on such discrepancies to enforce the reserve requirements. Currently the penalty is generally a charge equal to interest on the deficit at a rate equal to the discount rate plus 2 percentage points. The simplest alternative would be a fixed rate of "fine." To avoid discrepancies becoming an indirect form of discounting, the "fine" should be large enough to make it well above likely market rates of interest. The fine would then become the equivalent of a truly "penalty" discount rate—to use the language that was the source of so much discussion in the early days of the System—except that no collateral, or eligibility requirements, or the like would be involved.

An alternative to the complete abolition of discounting is to follow the Canadian precedent of tying the discount rate automatically to a market rate—currently the Canadian rate is set each week at ¼ of one percent above the latest average tender rate for Treasury bills. If the differential were sufficiently high, this would be equivalent to abolishing discounting. Otherwise, while such a device would eliminate some of the disadvantages I have enumerated, it would be decidedly inferior to the abolition of rediscounting, and would leave much room for the authorities to affect the discount rate through the amount of bills offered for sale, or similar devices if some other rate were used.

VARIATION IN RESERVE REQUIREMENTS

The power to vary reserve requirements is the most recent of the major monetary powers of the System. It was granted as an emergency power to be exercised only with the permission of the President in the Thomas Amendment to the Agricultural Adjustment Act of 1933 and then made a permanent power not dependent on Presidential permission in the Banking Act of 1935.

As was noted in the first chapter, the initial use of the power, in 1936 and 1937 to double reserve requirements in three steps, was drastic and most unfortunate. The mistake arose from a misinterpretation of the large amount of reserves in excess of legal requirements accumulated during the 1930's. The System regarded these excess reserves as a largely unintentional and passive accumulation by member banks arising out of a shortage of demand for loans or a short supply of acceptable bank investments. In consequence, it believed that raising legal reserve requirements would involve simply a relabelling of reserve balances and have no other current effect. In fact, it seems fairly clear, at least in retrospect, that the accumulation of excess reserves was largely motivated by a shift in liquidity preferences on the part of the banks. Bitter experience during the years from 1929 to 1933 had taught banks that it was not enough to keep in the form of high-powered money only the minimum amount required by law; legally required reserves could not be drawn on to meet emergency demands without the banks being liable to closure; and the ability to rediscount had proved an inadequate recourse for all too many banks. Little wonder that the survivors of the holocaust felt it necessary to provide their own protection against unexpected demands. Deposits in excess of required legal reserves were essentially uncovered liabilities for which only the excess of high-powered money over required reserves provided an effective reserve. True, the enactment of federal deposit insurance was to render unnecessary the maintenance of such a reserve, as was later the conversion of government securities into the equivalent of cash by the support program of the Federal Reserve. But at the time, deposit insurance was new and its effects unclear, and bond support still in the future. Doubling of required reserves was therefore much more than a change in labels; it reduced drastically the cushion of effective reserves, as the banks viewed them, available against these liabilities needing protection. As is strikingly clear from the detailed figures, the result was to induce banks to seek to rebuild their so-called excess reserves, thereby producing downward pressure on the money supply. The effects of the second and third steps in the rise in requirements were further intensified by the contemporaneous sterilization of gold by the Treasury.

This episode is an interesting example of how technical defects in a tool may greatly enhance mistakes in policy arising from erroneous analysis and thus play an independent role. Had the power to vary reserve requirements not been available, the System could have sought to reduce excess reserves by open market operations instead. Given its analysis of excess reserves, would it not have done so and thereby have produced the same deflationary effects? Rough calculation of the orders of magnitude involved makes it clear that the answer is no. The initial reserve requirement increase effective in August 1936 reduced excess reserves by about $1.5 billion and the second and third steps effective in March and May 1937 by another $1.5 billion. On the System's analysis that these reserves were excess in the economic as well as legal sense, it would have required open market sales of these amounts on the corresponding dates to achieve the same result. These amounts were exceedingly large relative to other magnitudes of the time. The $3 billion involved in the three steps together exceeded total government holdings of the Federal Reserve System by one-fifth and amounted to nearly one-quarter of total high-powered money in the hands of the bank and non-bank public. It is inconceivable that the System would have sought to sell $1.5 billion of securities in the course of a few weeks and then a further $1.5 billion in the course of two months only seven months later. And even if it had begun to do so, it would not have been committed to going through with the operation, as it was once a reserve requirement change was announced, and hence could have readily reversed course when the results became manifest.[6] The tool used was therefore not simply the means whereby a defective policy was put into effect but also affected materially the outcome in its own right.

A mistake of this kind is not likely to occur again. Excess reserves are now very small. The Reserve System now interprets changes in reserve requirements as more than a relabelling, acting as if an increase or decrease in excess reserves would tend to promote or retard expansion of earning assets by banks. It now recognizes their discontinuous effects, so that all reserve requirement changes since the end of the war have been accompanied by open market operations designed to offset the initial effect on reserve positions. Since 1951, all reserve requirement changes have been reductions, made when the System wished to promote ease. Nonetheless, variable reserve requirements are a technically defective instrument for controlling the stock of money and should be eliminated. If fractional reserves are to be retained, they should be set at a fixed level and kept there.

Variable reserve requirements share some of the same technical defects as discounting, and have additional defects of their own. A major one, as is clear from the discussion of the 1936–37 episode, is the fact that changes in reserve requirements are discontinuous in time and in practice have also been discontinuous in amount. The smallest change ever made is one-half of one percentage point. Applied to all member banks, this is a change of more than 4% of total required reserves —an amount that is larger than typical year-to-year changes in the absence of changes in requirements. It seems dubious that a policy instrument that proceeds by such large doses is desirable. There is no chance to see its effect or to adjust by small steps to effects different from those expected. Moreover, this defect is intensified by the difficulty of predicting how banks will react to changes in reserve requirements. The reaction of banks depends on many attendant circumstances, including their anticipation about whether the change in reserve requirements will be reversed or is a harbinger of further changes in the same direction.

Recognition of this defect of reserve requirement changes accounts, as mentioned above, for the Reserve System's postwar policy of accompanying reserve requirement changes with offsetting open market operations. Insofar as the open market operations initially offset the reserve requirement change fully, this would mean that changes in reserve requirements were being used not to affect the stock of money but simply to change the ratio of earning assets of banks to their total assets, that is, to alter the profitability of commercial banking. In practice, for reasons just noted, it is impossible to know what open market operations are required to fully offset a change in reserve requirements. The 1936 interpretation that a shift between excess reserves and required reserves has no effect is one extreme; it would call for no open market operations. The interpretation, now widely current, that a change in excess reserves has the same effect whether it arises out of a shift between required and excess reserves or out of a change in total reserves, is another extreme; it would call for open market sales or purchases equal in dollar amount to the amount of excess reserves released or absorbed. The correct interpretation is presumably between these two, its precise position depending on circumstances and varying from time to time. In consequence, the combination of a reserve requirement change and a supposedly offsetting open market operation is not "neutral" but introduces an expansionary or contractionary stimulus of uncertain and varying amount.

Changes in reserve requirements, like discount rate changes, are public and newsworthy, which means that they, too, have disturbing announcement effects and that there is strong resistance to reversing a change shortly after it is made if it does not have the expected effects or if economic conditions develop in an unexpected way. Further, it is not only difficult to predict the effect on the stock of money of changes in reserve requirements themselves but in addition such changes enhance the difficulty of predicting the effects of other factors such as gold movements, open market operations, and the like. Finally, changes in reserve requirements alter the profitability of commercial banking, which makes for a kind of pressure on the System that has nothing to do with its central function.

Aside from their variability, there are other features of reserve requirements that have monetary effects and need reform. Logically, this topic comes under the heading of banking reform that I shall discuss in the next chapter, but it is so intimately related to the control of the stock of money that some comment is necessary here. Moreover, my present comment will take for granted continuation of the present fractional reserve system while I shall there argue for its radical reconstruction.

Differences in reserve requirements among different classes of cities, as well as the failure to count vault cash as part of reserves, mean that changes in the distribution of deposits among cities tend to alter the total amount of money that is consistent with a given total of high-powered money. In consequence, here again the System must keep doing something in order to stay in the same place. It would simplify the System's task if these extraneous sources of changes in the money supply could be eliminated. As it happens, the two defects have tended partly to offset one another, since vault cash has tended to be higher for country than for reserve city banks and for reserve city than for central reserve city banks, whereas reserve requirements have differed in the opposite direction. It is therefore desirable that the two defects be removed simultaneously. The recently enacted authority to permit vault cash to be counted as reserves should be exercised, with offsetting changes in reserve requirements to avoid any net expansion or contraction in the stock of money. The recently enacted elimination of the differences between central reserve and reserve city banks in minimum and maximum reserve requirements is a step in the right direction and should be followed by a complete elimination of differences in actual requirements both between these two classes of banks and between them and country banks, again with offsetting changes designed to prevent any net effect on the stock of money. The differentiation in requirements among cities is a relic of the National Banking Act which made some sense at the time because deposits with banks in reserve and central reserve cities could be counted as reserves by other banks. It now has no such justification.

The different reserve requirements for demand and time deposits are another source of extraneous influences on the volume of money. This distinction was first introduced by the Federal Reserve Act. Prior to that time, reserve requirements were imposed on all deposits alike, whether demand or time. Evidence since then suggests that shifts between these categories have from time to time had their origin in pressures on reserves. Time deposits are of course different from demand deposits and by some definitions of "money" would not be treated as money but as a near-money. But this difference does not justify a difference in reserve requirements. The greater rate of use of demand than of time deposits may lead a bank holding both to expect greater variability in net withdrawals of demand than of time deposits and hence lead it to hold more liquid assets as the counterpart of its demand than of its time deposit liabilities. But, as we have seen earlier, required reserves do not perform this "banking" or "liquidity" function. Their function is very different. It is to enable the monetary authorities to control the stock of money. For this purpose, the differential requirements only complicate the task of the authorities. I would therefore urge that the present differentiation in the reserves required for time and demand deposits be eliminated, again, of course, with offsetting changes to avoid any net expansion or contraction in the stock of money.

CONCLUSION

The elimination of discounting and of variable reserve requirements would leave open market operations as *the* instrument of monetary policy proper. This is by all odds the most efficient instrument and has few of the defects of the others. It can be used continuously, from day to day, and in amounts varying by fine gradations. It need involve no public announcement, and thus there are neither announcement effects nor any obstacles to reversal of policy within a brief compass of time. It need involve no setting of rates of return or yields on securities, and does not directly affect the profitability of the banking business. It is highly impersonal and its effects are diffused over the banking community. The amount of purchases and sales can be at the option of the Federal Reserve System and hence the amount of high-powered money to be created thereby determined precisely. Of course, the ultimate effect of the purchases or sales on the final stock of money involves several additional links—what is happening to such other factors affecting high-powered money as the gold stock and Treasury balances; what is happening to the ratio between deposits and currency that the public is seeking to maintain; and what is happening to the ratio between deposits and reserves that banks are seeking to maintain. But the difficulty of predicting these links would be much less if rediscounting and variable reserve requirements were eliminated, and if reserve requirements were modified as I have suggested. The suggested reforms would therefore render the connection between Federal Reserve action and the changes in the money supply more direct and more predictable and eliminate extraneous influences on Reserve policy.

It has been said that open market operations are not themselves a fully general and impersonal tool because their effects depend on the kinds of securities purchased or sold. The restriction of purchases or sales to "bills only" since 1953 has been the most recent source of controversy. This range of problems is so intimately connected with debt policy that I shall defer it to the next chapter and consider it along with that problem.

One likely criticism of the proposals made in this chapter is that the streamlining of tools suggested involves reducing the "power" of the Federal Reserve System. Nothing could be farther from the truth. Retaining defective instruments of control which interfere with the operation of more efficient instruments does not mean retaining power any more than a marksman's ability to hit a distant target with a rifle would be enhanced by requiring him to shoot a blunderbuss at the same time with his left hand. On the contrary, by simplifying the System's instruments and making them better suited to the System's major functions, the reforms would increase its ability to achieve its objectives.

A frequent excuse for inadequacy of performance has been that the System lacked "power." So far as I can see there is only one episode on record for which this excuse is fully justified—the inflation resulting from large inflows of gold after the outbreak of the European War in 1914. On every other occasion, the inadequacy of performance has reflected either the adoption of an irrelevant or inappropriate objective or the failure to use power that was available. Except for the incident at the outbreak of World War I, there is no occasion since when the System lacked the technical power, or would have done so under the proposals I have made, to achieve any movements in the money supply that one might retrospectively have desired.

Chapter Three

Debt Management and Banking Reform

THE FIRST PART of this chapter deals with the one major tool of monetary policy that is outside the direct control of the Federal Reserve
System—debt management. It therefore completes the analysis of the
tools of monetary policy begun in the preceding chapter. The second
part of this chapter deals with banking reform. This topic is related to
the tools of monetary policy in general because these tools operate
largely through the banking system. It is related to debt management
in particular because the banks currently hold such a large amount of
government debt and would hold a far larger amount if the reforms
I shall suggest were adopted.

DEBT MANAGEMENT

The attention devoted to the "independence" of the Federal Reserve
System tends to obscure the essential fact that open market operations
and debt management are different names for the same monetary tool,
wielded in the one case by the Federal Reserve System, in the other,
by the Treasury. The fiction that the Federal Reserve System is only
quasi-governmental and its separation from the departmental organization of the federal administration no doubt alter the impact of political
influences and lead to different actions than would be taken if the
Reserve System were administratively consolidated with the Treasury.
As an economic matter, however, the accounts of the Federal Reserve

and the Treasury must be consolidated to determine what monetary action government is taking or to judge what the effects of such action are likely to be. A sale of government securities by the Federal Reserve makes the amount of high-powered money available for use as bank reserves or hand-to-hand currency less than it would otherwise be and thereby tends to make the stock of money less than otherwise. The sale of similar securities of the same total amount by the Treasury, with the proceeds added either to its balance with the Federal Reserve System or to its holdings of currency, has the identical effects. A purchase of securities by the Federal Reserve makes the amount of high-powered money available for use as bank reserves or hand-to-hand currency larger than otherwise and thereby tends to make the stock of money larger than otherwise. The redemption of similar securities of the same total amount by the Treasury out of its balance with the Reserve System or its holdings of currency has the identical effects. Similarly, a change in the maturity composition of the debt in the hands of the public can be achieved without a change in the amount of high-powered money either by offsetting Federal Reserve sales and purchases or by offsetting Treasury issue and redemption of securities, or, to go somewhat farther afield, by purchases or sales by the Exchange Equalization Fund or on behalf of trust funds under the control of the Treasury.

One unfortunate consequence for economic research of the confusion induced by the political separation of the Federal Reserve and the Treasury is the kind of statistical reporting it encourages. Federal Reserve accounts frequently tend to be consolidated or combined with those of commercial banks and other private agencies rather than with the accounts of the Treasury and other governmental agencies; this is generally done, for example, in tables showing the distribution of U.S. government obligations by holders.

A more serious consequence is the parallel confusion about the monetary effects of sales of government securities to commercial banks. It is alleged *ad nauseam* that such sales are "inflationary" in some sense in which sales of identical securities to the non-banking public are not. Although this fallacious view has other origins as well, in part it derives from the tendency to regard the Federal Reserve Banks as comparable to commercial banks rather than to the Treasury, and hence to attribute similar consequences to sales to commercial banks and to Federal Reserve Banks. A sale of securities by the Treasury to a Federal Reserve Bank is in economic effect no sale at all. It is simply an internal bookkeeping operation within the government incidental to the creation of money for current or future government use. When the Treasury spends the so-called "proceeds," it is simply spending the newly created money. The result is to add to the total of high-powered money and to create upward pressure on the money supply. A sale by the Treasury to the public is very different. It involves the transfer of funds from the public to the Treasury. The immediate monetary effect when the funds are added to the Treasury's balances at the Federal Reserve is identical with the effect of an open market sale by the Federal Reserve, and in the one case as in the other, tends to reduce the amount of high-powered money and to exert downward pressure on the money supply, and this is so whether the security is sold to a commercial bank or to a non-bank purchaser. When the Treasury spends the "proceeds," it restores the balances to the public, so that the end result of a sale of securities to the public, accompanied by an equal volume of expenditures, is to leave the money supply unaltered. This is so whether the securities are sold to a bank or a non-bank purchaser. The only monetary difference in the first instance is that a sale to a non-bank purchaser paid for by a check on a commercial bank account will reduce commercial bank deposits by the amount of the sale and thus required reserves by a fraction of the amount of the sale, while a sale to a bank will not reduce deposits. Allowance for further effects complicates the picture.

The view that sales of securities to commercial banks are inflationary is frequently defended on the grounds that commercial banks can "create" money to make the purchases. This argument is clearly invalid if the proceeds are to be added to Treasury balances at the Federal Reserve—commercial banks cannot "create" high-powered money. It is equally invalid if the proceeds are added to Treasury balances at commercial banks, when such deposits require the same reserves as other deposits. If the bank has no excess reserves, it can buy a government security only by disposing of some other investment or reducing loans outstanding—the Treasury gets a deposit instead of someone else. If the bank has excess reserves, either it is out of equilibrium, in which case, if it did not buy the government security, it would buy some other investment or make additional loans, or it desires excess reserves for liquidity purposes, in which case it will buy the security only if it can dispose of other assets. In either case, the Treasury gets a deposit instead of someone else. It is amusing how frequently the argument that sales to commercial banks are inflationary is combined with the argument that sales to Federal Reserve Banks are even worse because each dollar of Federal Reserve money gives rise to several dollars of deposits. The latter statement implies that reserves are fully used; but in that case there is not even a *prima facie* case for the argument that sales to commercial banks are inflationary in some sense in which sales to the non-bank public are not.[1]

One difference between open market operations of the Federal Reserve and debt management operations of the Treasury has just been alluded to. The Federal Reserve conducts its operations entirely through the use of high-powered money, which is to say, Federal Reserve notes or deposits; the Treasury keeps accounts also at commercial banks and conducts its operations at times in deposit money. A transfer of funds by the Treasury from commercial banks to Federal Reserve Banks or to its holdings of currency is like a decision by the public to convert deposits into currency and exerts downward pressure on the money supply, and conversely. The power to make such transfers can be and has been used as a monetary tool to alter the stock of money—not only in recent times but for decades before the Federal Reserve System was established. It is the one tool that is added to those discussed in the preceding chapter by widening our purview to include the Treasury. In recent times, its use has been produced largely by the tendency of the Treasury unlike the Reserve System to conduct its operations in large amounts at fairly widely separated dates. The "tax and loan accounts" and the device of spaced "calls" for transfer of funds to the Federal Reserve have developed to smooth the effect of these debt operations. Aside from this purpose, Treasury use of two different kinds of accounts, in commercial banks and in Federal Reserve Banks, involves the Treasury in independent monetary actions that are a source of instability unless coordinated with Federal Reserve actions. It seems better to concentrate responsibility in one agency. If an alternative method is adopted for smoothing Treasury debt operations, and I shall later suggest one, it would be desirable for the Treasury to rely predominantly on one kind of account, either reducing to minimum operating levels Treasury balances in commercial banks and as far as possible conducting all Treasury operations in high-powered money, or, alternatively, reducing the use of Federal Reserve balances and conducting Treasury operations as far as possible in deposit money.

Another difference is that the Federal Reserve creates and destroys high-powered money in performing its open market operations, whereas the Treasury in practice generally uses existing cash balances to redeem securities and adds proceeds of sales to its balances. But this difference is mostly in words. In terms of its effect on the public's cash balances, increasing or reducing Treasury balances of high-powered money is the economic equivalent of destroying or creating such money. Furthermore, the Treasury has at various times had the authority to create and destroy substantial amounts of high-powered money. It could currently create some $350 million by monetizing inactive gold and the so-called "seigniorage" silver, and from 1933 to 1945, it had the authority to issue $3 billion in United States notes.

As this example suggests, such differences as there are between Federal Reserve open market operations and Treasury debt management operations arise from different legislative limitations imposed on the two agencies, rather than from any difference in the economic character of the operations. Three are worth noting in addition to the difference between the authority to create money just referred to: (1) The Federal Reserve is not empowered to issue interest-bearing obligations of its own; in consequence, if at any time it should possess no earning assets, it would have no means available to reduce the total of high-powered money in use as hand-to-hand currency or bank reserves. It was recommended in the preceding chapter that the Federal Reserve be authorized to issue its own securities to remedy this limitation, although, as noted there, the limitation is most unlikely to be of practical significance in the near future. Under comparable circumstances, the Treasury might be able to issue securities and add the proceeds to its cash balances, depending on the specific legislative authorizations at the time. (2) The Federal Reserve is empowered to deal in a wider range of debt instruments than the Treasury. It can purchase and sell nonfederal obligations, such as acceptances and municipal warrants. (3) The Treasury is limited in the rate of interest that it is authorized to offer on securities having a maturity longer than five years, in the terms on which it can purchase or redeem outstanding issues before maturity, and in the total amount of debt it can create. The Federal Reserve is subject to no limitations with respect to the price at which it buys or sells.

It so happens that these limitations do not duplicate one another, so that by cooperating, as we shall see in more detail in a moment, the two agencies together are subject to hardly any effective limitations on the operations they can conduct in the federal debt, though of course political considerations may render it inexpedient to avoid limitations in this way.

The importance of consolidating Treasury debt management operations and Federal Reserve open market operations in judging the effect of monetary actions or policies can be illustrated by examining two monetary issues that have evoked controversy in recent months—the "bills only" policy of the Federal Reserve System which was adverted to at the end of the preceding chapter, and the legislative limitation of the rate of interest that the Treasury may offer on longer-term securities.

The "bills only" policy was adopted by the Open Market Committee of the Reserve System on March 5, 1953, when it declared that it would seek to limit its operations to Treasury bills, that is, to securities with a maturity of less than a year. If we neglect for the time being the legislative limitation on the rate of interest on long-term bonds and suppose that the Treasury can set any rate it wishes, then, so far as I can see, the "bills only" policy is essentially a device for allocating responsibility among different government agencies and imposes hardly any limits whatsoever upon the monetary actions that the Federal Reserve and the Treasury together can undertake. To avoid misunderstanding, let me hasten to state explicitly that I am not asserting that the monetary actions will in fact be the same whether the "bills only" policy is or is not maintained and followed. I am asserting rather that, if the monetary actions are different, it is not because they need technically to be, or because the "bills only" policy limits importantly the courses of action that are technically possible, but because a different allocation of responsibility among governmental agencies may lead to different actions. If I am right, the "bills only" policy may be important, but if so, hardly at all for the reasons that have been generally cited, and most of the arguments pro and con have been beside the main point. The crucial issue, if there be one, is whether this policy produces a proper administrative resolution of overlapping governmental jurisdiction, not whether it somehow puts undesirable limits on the possible scope of monetary action.

I can perhaps document these assertions most quickly by example. For succinctness, I shall speak somewhat loosely and not spell out each operation in full technical detail. Let us suppose that it is desired to add to high-powered money by reducing the amount of long-term securities in the hands of the public. In the absence of the "bills only" policy, the Federal Reserve could do this itself simply by buying long-term securities. Given the "bills only" policy, the same result can be accomplished by cooperation between the Federal Reserve and the Treasury: the Federal Reserve buys bills; the Treasury sells the same amount of bills and uses the proceeds to retire long-term securities. Alternatively, let us suppose that it is desired to reduce high-powered money by increasing the amount of long-term securities in the hands of the public. Under the "bills only" doctrine, the Reserve System will not sell such securities to the public directly; it sells bills instead. The Treasury sells the same amount of long-term securities and uses the proceeds to retire bills. In each case, the consolidated balance sheets of the Federal Reserve and the Treasury, on the one hand, and of the public at large, including of course commercial banks and other financial institutions, on the other, will be identical whether the operation is conducted by the Federal Reserve alone without the "bills only" policy, or by the Reserve and the Treasury together with that policy. In these terms, the "bills only" policy consists of assigning responsibility for the maturity distribution of the debt to the Treasury—an allocation of responsibility that seems eminently reasonable.

Let us now consider the legal limitation on interest rates, which we have so far neglected, and let us analyze its effect first in the absence of a "bills only" policy. As far as the consolidated balance sheet of the Federal Reserve and the Treasury is concerned, the limitation could be rendered nugatory by cooperation between the two agencies. Suppose it is desired to float a long-term issue but, in order to do so, it is necessary to pay a higher yield than the 4¼% interest coupon permitted by law. The Treasury can issue the security at terms permitted by law, sell it to the Federal Reserve, either directly or indirectly via market intermediaries, and the Federal Reserve can then resell the security or sell a comparable security from its portfolio at the market price. The capital loss the System would record is simply a bookkeeping entry which would serve to reduce the amount the System pays the Treasury out of Federal Reserve earnings, so that in this respect also the consolidated books of the Federal Reserve and the Treasury would be the same as if the Treasury had been able to conduct the operation directly. Again, let me emphasize that I am not saying that this will be done or should be done, but only that legally and technically it can be done.

If the "bills only" policy and the legal limitation on interest rates are simultaneously in effect, there is a reduction in the technical scope of monetary action—and it is, of course, this combination that has at bottom sparked recent controversy. The reason is that the kind of operation just outlined for avoiding the legal limitation on the interest coupon would be ruled out by the "bills only" policy. It is not clear that this is undesirable. I believe that the legal limitation on the interest coupon is exceedingly unwise. Given, however, that it has been explicitly legislated, is it really desirable to use "loopholes" to get around the clearly expressed intention of the legislature rather than to persuade the legislature that it is mistaken?

As these comments show, two problems must be faced in formulating a satisfactory debt policy: the administrative problem of coordinating the debt-management operations of the Treasury with the open market operations of the Federal Reserve and the economic problem of what the coordinated operations should be.

The technically most efficient arrangement for coordinating debt management with open market operations without a basic change in present institutional arrangements would be to assign full responsibility for debt management to the Federal Reserve. This would involve requiring the Treasury to acquire any funds it needs in excess of tax receipts by borrowing from the System and to use any excess receipts to repay its obligations to the System. It should be clear by now that in this context "borrowing" and "repayment" are purely bookkeeping fictions designed to keep interdepartmental arrangements in order. The System would then be responsible for buying and selling securities in accordance with monetary needs. It would be simpler if the securities it dealt in were obligations of the Federal Reserve System rather than of the Treasury, just as it would be simpler to have Federal Reserve notes as the sole paper money instead of our present conglomeration of United States notes, silver certificates, and Federal Reserve notes plus the other types in the process of retirement—and these changes should be made to unify both the interest-bearing and non-interest-bearing obligations of the U.S.[2] However, no great harm would be done by retaining present Treasury obligations, and even making new issues in the same form, as long as the Reserve System could determine the terms and amount of issue.

A technical reform along these lines runs precisely counter to present restrictions on transactions between the Treasury and the Reserve System.[3] The reason for these restrictions has been the belief that direct access by the Treasury to the System would increase the danger that the equivalent of the printing press would be used to finance governmental expenditures. I have much sympathy with the aim and it may be that the device of duplication of functions does promote it—this is a political problem of checks and balances which I have no special competence to judge. I must confess, however, to a sneaking suspicion that the duplication of responsibility under present arrangements is more conducive to "passing the buck" than to checking irresponsible behavior.

Though the technical reform just proposed seems clearly desirable, it is not essential to an effective co-ordination of policy. Moreover, it involves so superficially drastic a change in administrative arrangements, and runs so counter to many current beliefs, that it is hardly realistic to expect such a reform to be achieved in the near future, if ever. Accordingly, in discussing the substance of debt policy, I shall assume that no such reform is achieved, and that the Treasury continues actively to manage the details of issuing and retiring outstanding debt.

The main need with respect to debt policy seems to me to be the same as that which I emphasized in the preceding chapter with respect to the tools of monetary policy—to simplify and streamline, in such a way as to keep debt operations from themselves being a source of instability, and to ease the task of coordinating Treasury debt operations and Reserve open market operations.

Some steps have been taken in this direction, particularly in the handling of bills. In the main, however, actual debt policy has followed a different course. In the attempt to keep down the interest cost, and to achieve such other objectives as a wide distribution of securities and lengthened maturities, the Treasury has sought to "tailor" securities to the supposed demands of special groups of potential purchasers, and to time the issue of securities to fit into slack periods in the money market. The result has been a bewildering maze of securities of different maturities and terms, and lumpiness and discontinuity in debt operations, with refunding of major magnitude occurring on a few dates in the year. Instead of proceeding at a regular pace and in a standard way to which the market could adjust, debt management operations have been jerky, full of expedients and surprises, and unpredictable in their impact and outcome. As a result, they have been a continuing source of monetary uncertainty and instability. The most extreme examples in recent years are in the spring of 1953 and in the summer of 1958. The latter episode stimulated the recent joint Treasury-Reserve study of the government security markets. In typical human fashion, the two agencies concentrated on the mote in their brother's eye—supposed defects in the market for government securities—rather than on the beam in their own—the defects in the debt-issuing and monetary policies that were at bottom responsible for the speculation and subsequent difficulties associated with the 1958 refunding.[4]

The issuance of a wide variety of maturities has been justified on two main grounds: first, as a means of contributing to counter-cyclical forces; second, as a means of reducing government interest costs. Let us consider each in turn.

For counter-cyclical purposes, it is argued, the maturity of the debt should be lengthened in the boom to reduce the liquidity of the economy, and reduced in recession to increase liquidity. In practice, of course, this result has not been achieved. Since interest rates rise in boom and decline in recession, the temptation to borrow at short-term during the boom and fund in recession has been irresistible, producing changes in maturity precisely the opposite of those said to be desirable. Even if the desired changes could be produced, it is not clear that much would be gained. I rather suspect that the influence of minor changes in maturity on the demand for money is slight.[5] But, whether this is so or not, conversion of interest-bearing debt into non-interest-bearing is surely the same kind of device for promoting liquidity as the shortening of maturities and conversely, but one that is sharper and seems likely to be more consistent and predictable in its impact. And this is what is done by open market operations. Hence, shifts in maturity add nothing to open market operations.

The argument that tailoring issues is desirable to reduce interest costs has even less merit. It is entirely appropriate for the government to seek to borrow as cheaply as possible consistent with its other objectives. Though at first glance, tailoring securities to the needs of different groups of purchasers, and choosing the right time to issue securities, seem ways of achieving this objective, further examination renders this conclusion dubious. In the first place, the meaning of borrowing "as cheaply as possible consistent with its other objectives" turns out to be extremely complex. The relevant criterion is not total money interest payments to the public—these could be made zero simply by monetizing the debt, which is to say by producing an inflation, thereby imposing an implicit tax on holders of money and government debt and using the proceeds to pay off the interest-bearing debt. Nor is the relevant criterion the interest per dollar of debt, or the average interest rate.

For this would imply that the form of the debt had no effect on its amount, which is not likely to be true if one of the other objectives that constrains the minimization of cost is the avoidance of changes in the general level of prices, as it properly should be in the context of a debt policy. Let us suppose, for example, that short-term debt can be sold at a lower interest rate than long-term. It does not follow that it is cheaper in the relevant sense to sell short-term debt. Since short-term debt is a closer substitute for money than long-term, the amount of money that would be consistent with price stability if long-term debt were sold would imply rising prices if the same amount of short-term debt were sold instead. To avoid this outcome, the stock of money would have to be reduced by open market sales, which is to say, by issuing more debt. Thus a larger amount of short-term than of long-term debt would have to be sold, which might mean higher total interest costs. To put this point differently, it is necessary to take into account not only interest-bearing debt but also non-interest-bearing debt—Treasury currency and Federal Reserve notes and Federal Reserve deposits. By borrowing in the form of short-term securities instead of long, the government reduces the amount of real resources it can borrow at zero interest, and the gain on the one score must be offset against the loss on the other. But once this consideration is taken into account, it is clear that the minimization of cost is an exceedingly complex criterion. It is difficult if not impossible in the present state of knowledge to predict whether one or another pattern of securities will involve or did involve lower cost, correctly interpreted; hence there is no real basis for judging or improving performance.

A second and more fundamental objection to the argument that the tailoring of securities will reduce costs to the government is that this is equivalent to saying that the government can conduct a particular class of financial operations more cheaply than the market. Let the government issue only one maturity. Financial intermediaries will then arise that will convert this maturity into whatever maturities the market demands. Indeed, this is a major function of financial intermediaries— to reconcile the needs of lenders and borrowers by borrowing from the first on one set of terms and lending to the second on another. Why is this an activity which should be nationalized? Is not the argument that government should tailor its securities on a par with the argument that it should tailor clothes for its soldiers on the grounds that it wishes to acquire them as cheaply as possible? Is it not likely in the one case as in the other that it will get the relevant services more cheaply by buying them on the open market rather than by performing them through its own employees? Casual observation of government experience rather suggests that the answer is in the affirmative in the one field as in the other. Surely, the extensive profits that it has been possible to make through playing the pattern of rates and free-riding, as well as through speculation on issues that by the time subscriptions were due seemed wrongly priced, suggest that the government has been paying a high price for doing its own tailoring.

I can find no valid argument for the present policy of issuing a wide variety of securities and seeking to tailor their terms and date of issue to the market. And there is certainly much that is undesirable about that practice. It is a fertile source of confusion, uncertainty, and instability.

In suggesting an alternative that would avoid these problems, facilitate coordination with the Federal Reserve System, yet stay within the broad framework of present debt management arrangements, I shall assume that present administrative arrangements between the Treasury and the Federal Reserve remain basically unchanged, and also that the present fractional reserve banking structure is retained. If the banking reforms proposed later in this chapter were adopted, some modifications would be required. The alternative suggestion follows:

1. Retain the tap issues, mainly the savings bonds, in roughly their present form. These do little harm to an effective monetary policy since changes in the total amount outstanding proceed gradually.

2. Issue all remaining debt in two standard forms, one short-term to provide for seasonal needs, the other moderately long-term. The short security might be a 90-day bill or any other comparable maturity that was convenient. The longer-term security might best be a consol—that is, a perpetuity—but this is very much out of line with American experience. A less extreme break would be to make it, let us say, an eight- or ten-year maturity when issued. I do not myself believe that the precise maturity of the debt outstanding is of great significance. The length of the maturity does affect the demand for money and therefore has monetary implications. Depending on the maturity, the amount of money outstanding for a given price level, or alternatively the price level for a given amount of money, will differ. As long as this is a once-for-all effect it is of little importance and can be allowed for in the transition. The more important problem is to avoid continual erratic

shifts in the maturity distribution which will produce shifts in the price level to the extent that they are not offset by shifts in the money supply. For this reason, I regard limitation of debt instruments to a few highly stable types far more important than just what those limited types are.

Although the longer-term security would have a single maturity at date of issue, after some years the remaining maturity would vary from zero to the initial maturity. This would mean a gradual change in the average maturity during the transition period.

3. Sell both types of marketable securities at regular and frequent intervals—if feasible, weekly; if not, biweekly, or monthly. The amount to be sold each week or each month should be specified well in advance and should vary smoothly from one sale to the next. In order to avoid an undue number of separate issues, presumably some device can be adopted such as an open-ended issue. I do not however feel competent to outline details of this kind, important though they are. Even for the long-term issue it will doubtless not be possible to keep the amount sold the same or on a steady trend line from one week or month to the next but the aim should be to approximate this result. This will convert debt operations into a regular, steady, and predictable factor in the market. From the government's point of view, it will provide an automatic averaging device. The present policy of engaging in large operations at discontinuous intervals in effect forces the government to speculate on the course of market rates.

4. Sell both types of marketable securities only at auction. This will mean that the market will determine the price or yield and will eliminate any possibility of "free-riding." Current limitations on the interest rate that may be paid should be eliminated so as to give the market free rein.

5. Change the auction in one respect from that now used for bills. Currently, purchasers submit single bids for specified amounts and these are either accepted in whole or part or rejected. The result is that different purchasers may pay different prices for the same security. This practice establishes a strong tendency for the initial market to be limited to specialists and gives them a strong incentive to collude with respect to the bids submitted. Even casual examination of accepted bids each week and of the variation from week to week is enough to suggest that this tendency and this incentive have been effective. The range of bids accepted in any single auction is very narrow, frequently as narrow as the range between bid and ask quotations on comparable securities traded in the secondary market, and generally much less than the varia-

tion in the average bid from week to week, so much so that there is frequently no overlap from week to week in the accepted bids. A decidedly preferable alternative is to ask bidders to submit a schedule of the amounts that they will buy at a series of prices or of coupons; to combine these bids, and set the price or coupon rate at the level at which the amount demanded equals or exceeds the amount offered. One variant of this bidding technique that might be administratively simpler than the submission of schedules is to have the bid take the form of a *maximum* price that would be paid for a specified amount and, as now, to permit multiple bids. This would give identically the same result as the submission of schedules.[6] This alternative, in any of its variants, will make the price the same for all purchasers, reduce the incentive for collusion, and greatly widen the market. It is noteworthy that the Treasury's published objections to using the auction method for long-term securities all derive from the assumption that the present bill technique would be used and would be met fully by the alternative technique.[7]

A debt management policy along the lines of these principles would greatly ease the task of coordinating Reserve monetary operations with Treasury debt operations. Debt operations would be regular in timing, reasonably stable in amount, and predictable in form. The Reserve System could conduct its open market operations with a view to supplementing these debt operations so as to produce the desired effects on the money supply. Since the number of issues would be sharply limited, the market for each would be relatively broad, and the choice of which issues to buy and sell of no great importance. There would be no need for the succession of redemption crises that have become the pattern in recent years, or for the extensive consultation, crystal gazing, and plain guesswork that now go into setting coupon rates, maturities, and the like. Such a streamlining of debt management policy would be a fit companion for the streamlining of Federal Reserve tools proposed in the preceding chapter.

BANKING REFORM

As a student of Henry Simons and Lloyd Mints, I am naturally inclined to take the fractional reserve character of our commercial banking system as the focal point in a discussion of banking reform. I shall follow them also in recommending that the present system be replaced by one in which 100% reserves are required.[8] I shall depart from the original "Chicago Plan of Banking Reform" in only one respect, though one that I think is of great importance. I shall urge that interest be paid on the 100% reserves. This step will both improve the economic results yielded by the 100% reserve system, and also, as a necessary consequence, render the system less subject to the difficulties of avoidance that were the bug-a-boo of the earlier proposals.

DEFECTS OF PRESENT BANKING SYSTEM

Our present fractional reserve banking system has two major defects. First, it involves extensive governmental intervention into lending and investing activities that should preferably be left to the market. Second, decisions by holders of money about the form in which they want to hold money and by banks about the structure of their assets tend to affect the amount available to be held. This has often been referred to as the "inherent instability" of a fractional reserve system. Let us examine these two defects.

Government Intervention into Lending and Investing. For reasons suggested in the first chapter, governments have been led to intervene in lending and investing activities which have been combined with the issuance of fiduciary money to a far greater extent than in other lending and investing activities. Governmental supervision of banks and restrictions on their operations long predate any comparable supervision of other financial institutions, have always been more far-reaching, and continue to be so today. The valid concern with setting an external limit to the quantity of money and with preventing the economic equivalent of counterfeiting has led government to intervene into the arrangements among individuals with respect to borrowing and lending funds—an activity that is not a desirable function of government in a free society.

Governmental concern was initially concentrated on the issue of hand-to-hand currency. In this country, state bank notes were taxed out of existence just after the Civil War. The national bank notes then authorized were made the equivalent of a government obligation by requiring banks to have a reserve totalling more than 100% in the form of government bonds plus other currency.[9] In 1935, they were converted into a direct government obligation and are now in process of retirement.

The post-Civil War action rendered unnecessary supervision of the lending and investing activity of banks on account of their note issue. But deposits have since become a more important part of the circulating medium. Concern about them has led to an ever widening degree of control over the operations of commercial banks, of which the most recent and extensive is perhaps that associated with the federal insurance of deposits. The proposal to require 100% reserves for deposits involves applying the same policy to deposits that we have applied to currency.[10]

Inherent Instability. Under our present fractional reserve system, it is essential to distinguish the kind of money that can be used as hand-to-hand currency or as bank reserves—what I have called high-powered money—from deposit money, which I shall take to encompass deposits in commercial banks, whether labelled demand or time, recognizing that this is a somewhat arbitrary point at which to draw the line between "money" and "near-money." Currently, high-powered money consists predominantly of Treasury currency, Federal Reserve notes, and Federal Reserve deposits, with the Federal Reserve money in practice the only element subject to variation. For a given total of high-powered money in existence, a decision by a holder of money to convert deposits into currency tends to produce a decline in the total stock of money; a decision to convert currency into deposits, a rise. The reason is that each dollar of high-powered money in hand-to-hand circulation corresponds with a dollar of money in the hands of the non-banking public; each dollar in bank reserves with several dollars of deposit money. The same problem arises with respect to shifts among categories of deposits having different reserve requirements, which is the reason why I recommended in the preceding chapter that, whatever else was done, reserve requirements should be made uniform for all categories of deposits. Similarly, a change on the part of banks in the fraction of their assets they wish to hold in the form of high-powered money affects the number of dollars of deposit money per dollar of high-powered money and so alters the total stock of money.

These effects on the amount of money are unintended and incidental to the aims of the holders of money or the individual banker. They are side effects that have undesirable economic repercussions. As stated in the preceding chapter, the most extreme of these side effects—widespread liquidity crises involving runs on banks, banking panics, suspension of convertibility of deposits into currency, and, in the 1930-33 episode, drastic liquidation and ultimate collapse of the banking system —have now been rendered most unlikely by federal insurance of deposits. This amelioration of the one defect of fractional reserve banking was attained, however, only by exacerbating the other; federal insurance of deposits involves a substantial increase in governmental intervention into the lending and investing process.

Even aside from such extreme liquidity crises, the currency-deposit ratio and the deposit-reserve ratio are always experiencing changes that tend to produce perturbations in the behavior of the stock of money. In principle, the Federal Reserve can prevent these perturbations from occurring by introducing compensating changes into the stock of high-powered money. If the public decides to hold a larger ratio of currency to deposits, the Reserve System can create enough additional high-powered money through open market purchases to offset the effect on the total stock of money, and similarly with a shift in the reverse direction or with changes in banks' preferences. In practice, this is easier said than done. It is never possible to know what changes are going on until after the event, so that there is inevitably a lag in reaction, and further changes take place while the System is reacting. This is another case in which the System must act continuously in order to stay in the same place economically.

I do not want to overstate the technical problem of offsetting changes in the deposit-currency and deposit-reserve ratios. Aside from extreme liquidity crises, these ratios are relatively stable and change fairly gradually. Though their movements cannot be offset fully and instantaneously, they can be offset reasonably fully and reasonably promptly. If this has not been done consistently, it is less because the System has lacked the technical capacity than because it has not always taken the behavior of the money supply as a major criterion of policy or even as one of the principal guides to policy.

It is nonetheless a serious defect of our present fractional reserve system that it requires continuous jiggling of the monetary tools to offset individual choices that should have no influence on the stock of money The offsetting measures can never be perfect and hence the money supply behaves more irregularly than it needs to; moreover, at times, no offsetting is attempted and thus significant instability is introduced into monetary behavior.

POSSIBLE REMEDIES

To keep changes in the form in which the public holds its cash balances from affecting the amount there is to be held, the conditions of issue must be made the same for currency and deposits. This can be done by assimilating either the conditions for issuing currency to those that now prevail for deposits, or, conversely, the conditions for issuing deposits to those that now prevail for currency.

The first solution would involve permitting banks to issue currency as well as deposits subject to the same fractional reserve requirements and to restrict what is presently high-powered money to use as bank reserves—just as gold is now restricted to use exclusively as reserves for Federal Reserve notes and deposits, both of which now have the same gold reserve requirement. This solution would not, however, remove the effect of changes in the deposit-reserve ratio. Perhaps more important, it would greatly intensify the difficulty of preventing the economic equivalent of counterfeiting. After all, it was precisely the problems raised by note-issuing banks that led to the conversion of note issue to a governmental monopoly. And if required reserves were imposed on both deposits and notes to set an external limit on the amount of money and if past precedent prevailed, this solution would mean an expansion rather than a reduction of governmental intervention into lending and investing.

The alternative, which seems far preferable, is to assimilate the issue of deposits to that of currency. Currency is now a direct obligation of the government. It is at one and the same time money and high-powered money; for each dollar of currency there is a dollar of high-powered money; to speak figuratively, the issuance of currency requires a 100% reserve in the form of high-powered money. The counterpart for deposits would be to require any institution which accepts deposits payable on demand or transferable by check to have one dollar in high-powered money for every dollar in deposit liabilities (whether nominally demand or time deposits), that is, to have 100% reserves. The total of money and of high-powered money would then be the same. Shifts between deposits and currency would have no effect on the total stock of money and banks could not alter the ratio of deposits to reserves. The result would be to remove completely any instability in the stock of money arising from these sources. Since all money would in effect become a government obligation, there would be no need for federal insurance of bank deposits. 100% reserves would achieve its objectives more effectively and with less intervention into private activities.

HOW 100% RESERVES WOULD WORK

The effect of this proposal would be to require our present commercial banks to divide themselves into two separate institutions. One would be a pure depositary institution, a literal warehouse for money. It would accept deposits payable on demand or transferable by check. For every dollar of deposit liabilities, it would be required to have a dollar of high-powered money among its assets in the form, say, either of Federal Reserve notes or Federal Reserve deposits. This institution would have no funds, except the capital of its proprietors, which it could lend on the market. An increase in deposits would not provide it with funds to lend since it would be required to increase its assets in the form of high-powered money dollar for dollar. The other institution that would be formed would be an investment trust or brokerage firm. It would acquire capital by selling shares or debentures and would use the capital to make loans or acquire investments. Since it would have no power to create or destroy money, monetary considerations would not demand any special control over its activities. Hence, it need be subject to no more governmental supervision than other financial institutions.

TRANSITION TO 100% RESERVES

There is no technical problem of achieving a transition from our present system to 100% reserves easily, fairly speedily, and without any serious repercussions on financial or economic markets. Required reserves could be raised in a sequence of steps at dates specified in advance culminating in a final rise to 100% in, say, two years. The Reserve System would provide the additional reserves needed to prevent the increases in required reserves from reducing the stock of money by purchasing government securities on the open market. Reserve money created in this way would take the form of increased Federal Reserve deposits meeting the increased reserve requirements.

As of March 1959, commercial banks held deposits with the Federal Reserve Banks plus cash in vault, plus U.S. government securities totalling nearly 50% of the sum of their adjusted demand and time deposits. Until reserve requirements reached this level, all that would be involved would be essentially a bookkeeping operation—government securities would be replaced by a different government obligation, deposits at Reserve Banks. Thereafter, the funds acquired by non-bank holders of government securities would be available to purchase the assets that banks would have to dispose of to meet the additional reserve requirements or to purchase the capital stock and bonds issued by the investment trusts that banks would form to take over their lending and investing activities.

THE RELATION OF 100% RESERVES TO DEBT MANAGEMENT

This discussion of the transition brings out clearly the close connection between the 100% reserve plan and debt management. As of the end of March 1959, the direct and fully guaranteed interest-bearing debt of the federal government in the hands of the public—by which I mean outside both U.S. trust funds and the Federal Reserve System—totalled just over $200 billion, of which about $150 billion was in the form of marketable, $50 billion in non-marketable issues, mostly savings bonds. As of that date, the 100% reserve plan would have required commercial banks to add about $150 billion to their holdings of high-powered money. This is the amount of government securities the Reserve System would have had to buy to provide the additional reserves required. A hypothetical 100% reserve system in effect at that date would thus have involved the substitution of debt in the form of Federal Reserve notes and deposits, or, at one remove, of deposit liabilities of the depositary banks for practically the whole of the marketable government debt.

Subsequent increases in the stock of money could come either from the replacement of non-marketable securities by Federal Reserve deposits, or the creation of additional debt to finance deficits, or the acquisition by the Federal Reserve of assets other than direct or fully guaranteed obligations of the U.S. government. Possible assets that could be acquired include debt obligations insured or partly guaranteed by the federal government (like federally insured mortgages), obligations of states and municipalities, obligations of international organizations and of foreign governments, acceptances, and other commercial paper. Which alternative should be used and under what circumstances requires much more attention than I have given to it. Except for the replacement of non-marketable securities, which can serve for only a limited time, none on the surface is particularly appealing.[11]

WHY INTEREST SHOULD BE PAID ON RESERVES

One question that arises about the 100% reserve system is how the depositary institutions would get income to pay their expenses. The usual answer by proponents of 100% reserves is that they would get income solely by imposing service charges. I am disposed to add another source of income, namely, interest payments to the depositary institutions on their reserves. The interest would be paid by the govern-

72   A PROGRAM FOR MONETARY STABILITY

ment through the Federal Reserve System. This addition, which I hasten to add is not original with me,[12] seems to me to improve greatly the attractiveness of the 100% reserve plan.

Though the interest would be paid in the first instance to the banks, if competition prevailed—and there is every reason to permit entirely free entry into the business of providing depositary and check-clearing facilities—the receipts would be passed on to the depositors in the form either of interest paid on deposits or of services rendered without charge or at a charge below cost. In effect, the depositor would be combining lending funds to the government with holding cash balances, just as he now combines lending funds indirectly to both the government and to private bodies with holding cash balances in the form of bank deposits. As a bookkeeping matter, the Federal Reserve Banks would get the income to pay interest on their deposits from the interest received on the government securities they held, including those they purchased from banks and other investors in making the transition to 100% reserves. Economically, the government as a whole would get the funds to pay interest from the only sources available to finance any expenditures—taxation or borrowing.

The payment of interest on reserves has three related justifications, all of which are fundamentally part of a more general justification.

In the first place, as George Tolley has argued persuasively,[13] it would lead to a more nearly optimum stock of money in real terms. If money bears no interest, as hand-to-hand currency does not now and would not under the proposal, and as deposits would not under a 100% reserve plan in which no interest was paid on reserves, an individual must consider as the alternative cost of holding money the return he could receive on interest-bearing assets. For example, if one alternative is a government security yielding, say, 4%, the individual will seek to adjust his cash balances so that an additional dollar in cash would be worth just under 4 cents a year. To put it differently, it will pay him to spend up to 4 cents a year on productive services—if he is a merchant, for example, on an extra bookkeeper to enable him to match his receipts and expenditures more closely—for every dollar by which this will enable him to reduce his cash balances. But if money is a fiduciary currency, and so is essentially costless to produce, this is a waste of resources. It need cost society essentially nothing in real resources to provide the individual with the current services of an additional dollar in cash balances. The services of the bookkeeper are an inefficient way to get the equivalent of these services. If, therefore, assets that are equivalent to cash balances in respect of characteristics other than their usefulness as a medium of exchange pay a positive money rate of interest, there is a discrepancy between social and private costs that leads individuals to hold smaller than optimum cash balances and to devote more than the optimum amount of real resources to economizing cash balances.[14]

A complete solution would require either that all money bear interest, which is to say that fiduciary money be issued, as it were, only as a joint product with an interest-bearing security, or that the money rate of interest be zero, which could be achieved if prices fell at a rate equal to the real rate of interest. The latter solution is not clearly feasible as a practical matter. The former is feasible with respect to deposit money. It is achieved now to some extent through services rendered without charge and through the payment of interest on commercial bank deposits but to less than the optimum extent because of the non-interest-bearing reserves banks are required to keep, and because of the legal restrictions on the payment of interest on deposits. It would be achieved in full for deposit money by the proposed 100% reserve arrangement if interest were paid on these reserves, and banks were free to pay any rate of interest they wished on deposits. Although at various times in the past interest-bearing notes have circulated as currency,[15] the practical problems involved seem too great to make it feasible to pay interest on hand-to-hand currency. The payment of interest on deposit money alone would lead to a higher than optimum ratio of deposits to currency. It seems dubious, however, that this loss could offset more than part of the gain from the more nearly optimum incentive to hold deposits.

The second justification for paying interest on reserves is a highly practical counterpart to the abstract argument just presented. One objection that has always been raised, with some justification, against other versions of the 100% reserve plan, is the existence of a strong incentive to evade the requirement of 100% reserve. Much ingenuity might thus be devoted to giving medium-of-exchange qualities to near-monies that did not qualify under the letter of the law as deposits requiring 100% reserves. As a result, the stabilizing effect of the 100% reserve plan would be reduced. In addition, the prevention of evasion would involve extensive governmental intervention into private financial arrangements. The incentive to evade 100% reserves arises precisely because of the discrepancy that exists between private and social costs when money bears no interest and near-monies do. If interest is paid on the 100% reserves, the incentive to evade the reserve requirement is largely if not wholly eliminated. There is now little or no profit to be made in finding ways to attach medium-of-exchange qualities to near-money. In consequence, the problem of enforcing the 100% reserve arrangement is vastly simplified and need involve no intervention into other private financial arrangements.

The third justification for paying interest on reserves is on grounds of equity. It is not easy to see why the government should pay an annual fee for the resources it borrows from some individuals, namely, the holders of interest-bearing government securities, and nothing for the resources it borrows from other individuals, namely the holders of money now and under the 100% reserve arrangement.

The reason why the government can discriminate between the two classes of lenders brings us to the common source of these three justifications for the payment of interest on reserves: the technical monopoly character of a fiduciary money stressed in the first chapter. The government has no monopoly on the issuance of interest-bearing securities; hence it must pay the competitive market rate to borrow in that form. It has a monopoly on the issuance of money, though it has chosen to give up part of its monopoly powers by permitting commercial banks to operate with fractional required reserves. It can therefore borrow at a price that yields it a monopoly return—in this case by paying a zero interest rate. In general, as is well recognized, the optimum price for the product of a technical monopoly operating under conditions of constant cost is a price equal to marginal cost. In the present instance, the production of fiduciary money is a technical monopoly operating under conditions of roughly constant cost. The marginal cost for reserve money is essentially zero. For deposit money, it is the cost of the depository and check-clearing services. The cost to the holder is now greater than this, since he must give up the interest he could receive on other assets. The payment of interest on reserves to banks, and of interest received by banks less the costs of operation to depositors, would therefore involve pricing the monopoly product at marginal cost.

The case for payment of interest on reserves applies not only to the 100% reserve system, but equally to our present fractional reserve system. Accordingly, even if reserves are not raised to 100%, Reserve Banks should be required to pay interest on their deposit liabilities.

Currently, they indirectly do so to a limited extent by bearing some of the costs of check-clearing and other services activities. It would be far better for them to pay interest directly and to charge for any services they now render free. Of course, the payment of interest on reserves would render it especially urgent to eliminate present restrictions on the interest that banks may pay their depositors.

HOW INTEREST PAYMENTS ON RESERVES MIGHT BE DETERMINED

Granted that Federal Reserve Banks should pay interest on their deposit liabilities, how much should they pay? My first thought was that the rate of interest should be equal to the average yield on relatively short-term marketable government securities—perhaps the yield on the weekly or monthly auction of bills suggested above, and that it should vary from week to week or month to month along with that yield. This device would be entirely reasonable for determining the interest to be paid on existing reserves. However, the figures cited above on the magnitudes involved in passing to 100% reserves make it clear that it would not be reasonable for the greatly enlarged reserves involved in the 100% reserve plan—the tail would wag the dog. The only alternative that seems at all feasible is to set the initial rate at a level equal to the average yield on short-term government issues, during, say, the preceding several months, and then to vary it every quarter or every six months, in accordance with changes in the yield of short-term private obligations such as 90-day commercial paper. This problem of how to set the rate of interest is another issue that I feel most uncertain about and that requires more attention than I have given to it.

CONCLUSION

In closing this discussion of banking reform, I should like to quote from a talk I gave some years ago. "For a long time," I said in 1954, "I have been a proponent of 100% reserve banking. . . . Those of us who favor this scheme are accustomed to being labelled 'unrealistic'; to being told that we are proposing a reform that has no chance of adoption and would require utterly impractical changes in the banking system if it were adopted. Yet, ironically enough, a completely unnoticed effect of the changes in bank assets [during and after the war] has been to take us half the way to complete adoption of the plan. For the essence of the plan is precisely to make all money, whether currency or deposits, a direct liability of the government issued under uniform arrangements." But already, roughly "half the deposits of the public [in commercial banks] are government liabilities at one remove, in the sense that the bank assets corresponding to them are government liabilities," either in the non-interest-bearing form of currency or Federal Reserve deposits, or in the interest-bearing form of government securities. "For this half, Federal deposit insurance simply gilds the lily and makes them a government liability twice over." [16]

Chapter Four

The Goals and Criteria of
Monetary Policy

WE ARE NOW all dressed up. Where should we go? Toward what end and in what way should we use the streamlined monetary mechanism outlined in the preceding chapters, or for that matter, our present antiquated, creaking model?

Since at least John Maynard Keynes' tract on *Monetary Reform*,[1] it has been a commonplace that this problem has two sides, the international and the internal, and that the solution adopted for the one may narrowly limit the alternatives available for the other. It so happens that these two sides come closer to being independent for the United States under present conditions than for most other countries and for most other times. Moreover, the international monetary arrangements that seem to me best leave a maximum of leeway with respect to internal policies. For these reasons, as well as the heightened interest in the problem produced by the recent declines in the U.S. gold stock, I shall consider international relations first and then turn to internal policy.

INTERNATIONAL MONETARY RELATIONS

A small country on a commodity standard that is common to much of the rest of the world—or, what is economically the same thing, that seeks to maintain fixed rates of exchange between its own currency and the currencies of most other countries without using foreign exchange controls or their equivalent—has little leeway with respect to internal monetary policy. Its stock of money must be whatever is required to maintain external equilibrium. Internal policies and events affect internal monetary conditions primarily through their effect on the demand for and supply of foreign exchange and hence on the behavior of the stock of money that is required to maintain external equilibrium.

For most of the period prior to World War I, the United States was in this situation. Our internal price level and our internal stock of money were dominated by world-wide movements in prices and by international flows of capital that together determined the price level in the United States consistent with external equilibrium. The only important exception was the period from 1862 to 1879, when the United States was on an inconvertible paper standard with flexible exchange rates and so could follow an independent internal monetary policy. Yet even the latter part of this period was dominated by the desire to resume gold payments at prewar exchange rates. In the two other periods of great instability referred to in the first chapter—1837–44 and the mid-1890's—monetary uncertainty created difficulty mostly through its effects on our international position. In both cases, doubts about the maintenance of the commodity standard led to recurrent flights from the dollar, which is to say, to speculative capital movements, and affected other capital movements as well. The capital outflow, or reduction in capital inflow, made the internal price level consistent with maintenance of the standard lower that it would otherwise have been. The standard could be maintained, as in both cases it was albeit with some lapses, only by accepting a more severe internal deflation than would otherwise have been necessary. For the rest of the period up to World War I, it involves only mild overstatement to say that internal monetary arrangements had little or no effect on the size of the changes in the money supply that occurred. Their impact was rather on the channels through which such changes as did occur took place, and on the composition of the money supply.

Since World War I, the situation has been very different. Except for the period from March 1933 to January 1934, when, as in the greenback period, we were on an inconvertible paper standard with flexible exchange rates, we have nominally been on a gold standard, though of a different character and at a different parity after 1934 than before. Yet internal monetary behavior has been dominated by external forces on at most three occasions—in 1920–21, when the rapid approach of the Federal Reserve's gold-reserve ratio to its legal minimum triggered the sharp rise in the discount rate in January 1920 that set off or intensified the subsequent internal deflation, and when an easing of policy was postponed until the ratio had reversed its movement and seemed safely above its legal minimum; for the second time in 1931, when Britain's departure from the gold standard and the fear of an outflow of gold triggered the sharp rises in the discount rate in October 1931 that intensified the internal deflation; and, for the third time, in the period from 1934 to 1939, when the rise in the official U.S. price of gold in January 1934, combined with a capital flight from Europe in the wake of Hitler's accession to power, produced large flows of gold to the United States which were the major source of the contemporaneous growth in the stock of money. And even this last episode is somewhat dubious. If gold flows had not produced an expansion in the stock of money, it seems highly likely that a similar expansion would have been produced by other measures, since domestic policies so clearly aimed at an increase. For the rest of the period since 1914, it is hard to see any close connection between the internal behavior of the money supply and the needs of external equilibrium. External forces have manifested themselves primarily in changes in foreign holdings of dollar balances or in movements in the gold stock that have been offset by the monetary authorities—"sterilized," to use that antiseptic term which seems ironically appropriate in view of the contagiousness of the disease that resulted on two of the three occasions when gold flows were reacted to rather than offset.

There are several reasons why the United States has been able to achieve so large an apparent degree of independence in its internal monetary behavior during this period. One is that for much of the period most other countries of the world have not been on the gold standard. As far as exchange rates are concerned, it does not matter whether the dollar price of gold is free to vary and the price in foreign currency fixed, as was the case for example, in the greenback period, or whether the dollar price is fixed and the foreign price free to vary, as was the case for many countries for some years after World War I and World War II and during much of the 1930's and is now, for example, for Canada. In either case, variable exchange rates provide a means of reconciling external equilibrium with independent internal monetary policies. Another reason is the asymmetry that we, like most other countries, have displayed with respect to surpluses and deficits in our external accounts. During most of the period since World War I, it so happened that economic circumstances, our policies, and the policies of other countries produced an actual or potential surplus in our balance of payments. Prior to 1914, the resulting inflow of gold would have tended to produce increases in the money supply and this tendency would have been permitted to operate. After 1918, the monetary authorities could more readily prevent similar tendencies from being effective and were more inclined to do so. We have been willing to accept gold inflows passively and to let our gold stock grow. We have reacted very differently to gold outflows. The two clear cases in which external forces affected internal monetary behavior both involved reactions to actual or potential outflows, even though, in both cases, gold stocks were at historic highs as a result of prior gold inflows. And again in the past several years, much more concern has been expressed about gold outflows than was ever expressed about the preceding gold inflows that raised gold stocks to unprecedented levels.

Both reasons come down to one basic explanation for our large measure of independence in monetary policy despite our nominal adherence to a gold standard: the rest of the world has been largely adapting to us rather than we to them. We have become so large a part of the world that our policies have important effects on worldwide trends. Moreover, foreign payments bulk larger in the accounts of most other countries than in our own. Other countries, too, display asymmetric reactions to surpluses and deficits; our passive acceptance of gold inflows has simply thrown the necessity of adjustment on them. They too have frequently been willing to accept gold inflows—witness France in the late 1920's or Germany in recent years—but have reacted to outflows. The incompatibility of fixed exchange rates with independent monetary policies that Keynes analyzed so brilliantly has been manifested, but we have mostly been the silent partner. The measures adopted by other countries as a result of this incompatibility have varied widely, depending on internal attitudes and policies and on the other problems they faced: flexible exchange rates, adopted widely after World War I and again in the later 1930's; the alteration of internal policies, attempted in Britain to some extent after 1925 and by many countries in the Great Depression; direct control of foreign exchange transactions, adopted widely after World War II; and so on.

Our domestic policies have of course not been completely independent of our foreign payments position. For example, the so-called "dollar shortage" in the postwar years doubtless made our outlays on foreign aid larger than they would otherwise have been, just as now the outflow of gold is producing some pressure to reduce foreign-aid expenditures. But the connection has been weak, and, more important for our purposes, has not taken the form, enshrined as the classical gold-standard mechanism of adjustment, of automatic adaptation of the stock of money to the needs of external equilibrium.

A full-fledged gold standard in which all money consisted of gold or warehouse receipts for gold except perhaps for a fixed fiduciary issue would have the great merits of complete automaticity and of freedom from governmental control. It would be costly in terms both of resources used to mine gold and of the price movements resulting from changes in the relative cost of producing gold and other commodities. Nonetheless, if it were feasible, the advantages might be well worth the cost. For reasons suggested in the first chapter, however, it seems dubious that such a monetary system is stable. It is not the system supported by most current proponents of the gold standard nor is it the system that prevailed even during the halcyon days of the gold standard in the nineteenth century, when there were large admixtures of fiduciary elements and much conscious management. It is even farther from the nominal gold standard that prevailed in the United States from World War I to 1933, let alone since 1934. During that period we have had none of the advantages of a full-fledged gold standard, and many of its disadvantages greatly exaggerated.

Only a cultural lag leads us still to think of gold as the central element in our monetary system. A more accurate description of the role of gold in U.S. policy is that it is primarily a commodity whose price is supported, like wheat or other agricultural products, rather than the key to our monetary system. Our price support program for gold differs in three important respects from our price support program for wheat: first, we pay the support price to foreign as well as domestic producers; second, we sell freely at the support price only to foreign purchasers and not to domestic; third, and this is one important relic of the monetary role of gold, the Treasury is authorized to create money to pay for gold it buys so that expenditures for the purchase of gold do not appear in the budget and the sums required need not be explicitly appropriated by Congress. This final characteristic has applied equally and for the same reason to our purchase of silver under the various price support programs that have been in effect since 1934. We have accumulated gold in the past until we now hold half the world's gold for the same reason that we have accumulated wheat—because the support price of $35 an ounce has been above the market price. In these terms, should we not welcome a situation that enables us to dispose of some part of this particular surplus?

Gold has one additional role. The Reserve System is required by law to keep a reserve in gold equal to 25% of its liabilities for Federal Reserve notes and deposits. Present reserves are well above this level and are likely to continue to be under circumstances now foreseeable. But if they should approach the 25% limit, it seems likely that the limit would be changed, as occurred when the former limits were approached in 1945, rather than the reserve position being allowed to force a monetary deflation not otherwise welcome—and this is certainly the desirable course of events. Hence, even as a monetary reserve, gold is primarily a symbol.

Since early 1958, our gold stock has declined some three billion dollars. There is no way of identifying this decline with any particular element of our balance of payments. It is simply the form in which foreigners have chosen to take part of the excess of their dollar receipts from U.S. purchases of goods and services, capital investments abroad, private gifts, and government foreign aid over their dollar expenditures on the corresponding items. So long as our present gold policy is maintained, gold is the equivalent of dollars to foreign holders. It may be preferred, either because its price is expected to rise or because it is desired for use as monetary reserves by other countries or as monetary hoards by individuals.

Because foreign aid is an independent source of dollars determined by non-market forces, there has been some tendency to link the loss of gold with foreign aid. In these terms, one might describe the loss of gold by saying that the rest of the world has decided to take a large part of the foreign aid that we have been giving them in the form of gold rather than of other goods. From our point of view, the gold in Fort Knox is serving no productive function; we use it for neither food, nor clothing, nor housing. The goods that foreign countries might take instead are contributing to our welfare. In consequence, it is very much to our interest to have foreign aid take the form of the export of gold rather than of goods. We accumulated much of the gold during and after the war because foreign countries had an urgent need for American goods in excess of the amount they could buy with dollars they earned, borrowed, or received as aid. We did not then allow the inflow of gold to influence our domestic monetary policy. It would be a mistake to allow the outflow of gold now to do so.

I see little justification for continuing our present gold policy. We are not prepared, and in my view rightly, to permit gold flows to dominate internal monetary policy. And it is hard to see why gold is a commodity whose price we should support. The chief gold producing countries are South Africa, Canada, and the U.S.S.R.; none is a country that we have felt it important to assist by economic aid; if we did want to assist them, it would be cheaper and more effective to do so by direct grants of aid; and this is certainly the case for gold mining interests in our own country.

The present gold drain offers an opportunity to reduce our stockpile of gold. It also has some value in contributing to the removal or reduction of discriminatory trade barriers or foreign exchange restrictions that have been erected by some foreign countries against goods from the United States. On the other hand, it raises the serious danger that, if the drain continues, the pressure to do something about it will lead us to take measures that are undesirable—either to raise the price of gold, thereby still further increasing the cost of the gold-support program, or to impose additional impediments to imports and stimulate exports, thereby departing still further from the free trade policy toward which we should be moving, or to tighten monetary policy more than is required for internal reasons. The way to avoid being forced into any of these measures is to cease offering to buy and sell gold at a fixed price, to eliminate the present anachronistic gold reserve requirements, and to allow the price of gold to be determined in the free markets of the world. At the same time, we should also abandon the even less justifiable commitments to purchase silver.

It is tempting to believe that the present outflow of gold means that if our price support program were eliminated the free market price of gold would rise above $35 an ounce. This might well be the case but it is by no means clear that it would be. A major reason why foreigners and others wish to hold gold is because it is convertible into dollars at a fixed price. The real demand is for dollars. If we abandoned support of the price of gold, but, let us say, retained our present stock, the demand for gold would be altered since gold would no longer have the property of conferring command over a fixed number of dollars. The result might be a decline rather than a rise in the world price of gold.

As matters now stand, the fixed gold price of $35 per ounce serves to determine exchange rates between the dollar and the currencies of other countries that also maintain a fixed price for gold. Although abandoning the fixed price for gold could be combined with rigid exchange rates through other devices, it would be far better, in my view, to allow the rates of exchange to be determined by the market. This would require that the U.S. refrain both from setting any official rates of exchange between the dollar and other currencies and from governmental speculation in exchange markets. This is essentially the arrangement that Canada adopted some years ago and that has been working well since. I have elsewhere outlined at some length the case for a system of flexible exchange rates.[2] It will suffice here, therefore, to say that such a system permits a maximum degree of international cooperation among countries, each separately following an independent internal monetary policy, without requiring exchange controls, import or export quotas, or other impediments to trade.

INTERNAL MONETARY POLICY

Given that we are not and should not be prepared to permit internal monetary policy to be dominated by either gold flows or other manifestations of foreign payment arrangements, there remains the central question: what is to be our internal monetary policy?

In a celebrated article on "Rules versus Authorities in Monetary Policy," [3] Henry Simons contrasted sharply two ways of answering this question: one, by specifying a general goal and then giving monetary authorities wide powers to use at their discretion in promoting it; the other, by assigning specific responsibilities to monetary authorities to be carried out in accordance with rules specified in advance and known to all. As Simons made clear, the contrast is not complete. The general goal alone limits somewhat the discretion of the authorities and the powers assigned to them do so to an even greater extent; and reasonable rules are hardly capable of being written that do not leave some measure of discretion. Yet the contrast is nonetheless both marked and important.

In practice, we have relied almost wholly on authorities. As was pointed out in an earlier chapter, we have done so not by intention but because the change in the role of the gold standard brought about by

World War I loosened so greatly what the authors of the Federal Reserve Act had expected to be the effective "rule" limiting the discretion of the monetary authorities. In the absence of the strait-jacket of a rigid gold standard, "accommodating commerce and business," to quote the original Federal Reserve Act, imposed hardly any restrictions on the discretion of the authorities.[4]

Relying so largely on the discretion of authorities in so important an area of policy is highly objectionable on political grounds in a free society. Experience has demonstrated that it has also had unfortunate monetary consequences. It has meant continual and unpredictable shifts in the immediate guides to policy and in the content of policy as the persons and attitudes dominating the authorities have changed—from the "real bills" emphasis of the early 1920's to the offsetting of inventory speculation of the mid-20's to the restraint of stock market speculation of the late '20's to the sensitivity to external pressures and timidity in face of internal drains of the early '30's, to the bond-support policies of the '40's, to the sensitivity to cyclical movements and reliance on "announcement effects" of the '50's. It has meant continual exposure of the authorities to political and economic pressures and to the deceptive effects of short-lived tides of events and opinions. The role of the monetary authorities is to provide a stable monetary background, to go counter to or at least not reinforce the ever shifting tides of current opinion and events. This is the justification for their alleged "independence." Yet the vagueness of their responsibilities and the wide range of their discretion has left them no means other than "wisdom" and personal perspective of withstanding contemporaneous pressures and has denied them the bulwark that clearly assigned responsibilities and definite rules would have provided.

Reliance on discretion in pursuing general goals has meant also the absence of any satisfactory criteria for judging performance. This has made it nearly impossible to assess responsibility for success or failure and has greatly enhanced the difficulty of learning by experience. The Reserve System, or even monetary authorities more broadly defined, have not been the sole agencies responsible for the general goals that they have sought to promote, and that have become the current translation of "sound credit conditions and the accommodation of commerce, industry, and agriculture"—such general goals as economic stability, full employment, price stability, growth. These goals are to be approached through the joint actions of many public and private agencies, of which monetary authorities are only one. Success or failure in achieving them cannot be attributed to monetary policy alone, and hence cannot be a criterion of performance. An amusing dividend from reading *Annual Reports* of the Federal Reserve System *seriatim* is the sharp cyclical pattern that emerges in the potency attributed to monetary forces and policy. In years of prosperity, monetary policy is a potent instrument, the skillful handling of which deserves credit for the favorable course of events; in years of adversity, other forces are the important sources of economic change, monetary policy has little leeway, and only the skillful handling of the exceedingly limited powers available prevented conditions from being even worse.[5]

The granting of wide and important responsibilities that are neither limited by clearly defined rules for guiding policy nor subject to test by external criteria of performance is a serious defect of our present monetary arrangements. It renders monetary policy a potential source of uncertainty and instability. It also gives greater power to the men in charge for good or ill, greater "flexibility" to meet problems as they arise, to use the phrase that the Reserve System likes to emphasize. If the analysis presented in the first chapter has any large measure of validity, experience suggests that eliminating the danger of instability and uncertainty of policy is far more urgent than preserving "flexibility." The major need in reforming our present control of monetary policy is, therefore, to provide more definite guides to policy and more satisfactory criteria of performance.

One way to do so that has frequently been urged is to adopt price level stability as simultaneously the specific goal for monetary policy, the immediate guide to policy, and the criterion of performance. There is much to recommend price level stability as the specific goal of monetary policy, as the way to separate the special role of monetary policy from that of other segments of economic policy in furthering our more nearly ultimate goals. The stock of money has a critical influence on the price level. No *substantial* movements in the price level within fairly short periods have occurred without movements in the same direction in the stock of money, and it seems highly dubious that they could. Over long periods, changes in the stock of money can in principle offset or reinforce other factors sufficiently to dominate trends in the price level.

I share, however, the doubts that the Reserve System has repeatedly expressed about the desirability of using price level stability as an immediate guide to policy. Entirely aside from the technical problem of the specific index number of prices that should be used, the key difficulty is that the link between price changes and monetary changes over short periods is too loose and too imperfectly known to make price level stability an objective and reasonably unambiguous guide to policy.

The Federal Reserve System does not control the price level. It controls the volume of its own earning assets and, at one remove under present circumstances or directly under the altered arrangements suggested in the preceding chapters, the stock of money. If the link between the stock of money and the price level were direct and rigid, or if indirect and variable, fully understood, this would be a distinction without a difference; the control of the one would imply control of the other; and it would be indifferent whether the guide to policy was stated in terms of the end to be achieved, stability of the price level, or the means to be used, changes in the stock of money. But the link is not direct and rigid, nor is it fully understood. While the stock of money is systematically related to the price level *on the average,* there is much variation in the relation over short periods of time and especially for the mild movements in both money and prices that characterize most of our experience and that we would like to have characterize all. Even the variability in the relation between money and prices would not be decisive if the link, though variable, were synchronous so that current changes in the stock of money had their full effect on economic conditions and on the price level instantaneously or with only a short lag. For it might then be fairly easy to substitute trial and error for a full understanding of the link between money and prices. Mistakes would not be cumulative and could be corrected quickly. In fact, however, there is much evidence that monetary changes have their effect only after a considerable lag and over a long period and that the lag is rather variable. In the National Bureau study on which I have been collaborating with Mrs. Schwartz, we have found that, on the average of 18 cycles, peaks in the rate of change in the stock of money tend to precede peaks in general business by about 16 months and troughs in the rate of change in the stock of money to precede troughs in general business by about 12 months. The results would be roughly comparable if the comparisons were made with peaks and troughs in a price index rather than in general business. For individual cycles, the recorded lead has varied between 6 and 29 months at peaks and between 4 and 22 months at troughs. This is highly consistent behavior as such observations go and sufficient to pin down the *average* lead within a rather narrow range. But it is highly variable behavior for the individual episode with which policy must be concerned.

Under these circumstances, the price level—or for that matter any other set of economic indicators—could be an effective guide only if it were possible to predict, first, the effects of non-monetary factors on the price level for a considerable period of time in the future, second, the length of time it will take in each particular instance for monetary actions to have their effect, and third, the amount of effect of alternative monetary actions. In the present state of our knowledge, it is hard enough to conceive of an effective trial-and-error procedure for adapting to price level movements of two, three, or four years in length if monetary action taken today uniformly had its effect over a period centered, say, 14 months from now. I find it virtually impossible to conceive of an effective procedure when there is little basis for knowing whether the lag between action and effect will be 4 months or 29 months or somewhere in between. We are probably only today experiencing the effects of the rapid expansion in the money supply in the first half of 1958 in response to the 1957–58 recession. That recession itself may well have reflected in part the relatively slow rate of increase during 1956 and 1957, in its turn a reaction to the contemporaneous rise in prices. The 1956–57 price rise was itself related to the monetary expansion in 1954 and 1955 which was a reaction to the recession of 1953–54; and so on. Though oversimplified, this portrayal has enough potential validity to illustrate the problem.

A satisfactory policy guide or rule should be connected more directly with the means available to the monetary authority than is the price level. We will, I believe, further the ultimate end of achieving a reasonably stable price level better by specifying the role of the monetary authorities in terms of magnitudes they effectively control and for whose behavior they can properly be held responsible than by instructing them solely to do the right thing at the right time when there is no clear and accepted criterion even after the event whether they have done so. In this as in so many human activities what seems the long way round may be the short way home.

The most important magnitude that the monetary authorities can effectively control and for which they have primary responsibility is the stock of money. Under present circumstances, even the stock of money is not directly controlled by the System. The System controls directly its own earning assets. As we have seen, the total of high-powered money is affected in addition by such factors as gold flows, changes in Treasury balances, and the like; and the total money stock for any given total of high-powered money is affected by the ratio of high-powered money to deposits that banks choose to hold and the ratio of currency to deposits that the public chooses to hold. These slips between control of earning assets and of the stock of money would be largely eliminated by the reforms proposed in the preceding chapters. These reforms would make changes in the earning assets of the Reserve System essentially identical with changes in the money supply and thereby give the System direct control over the money supply. But even under present circumstances, the links between Reserve action and the money supply are sufficiently close, the effects occur sufficiently rapidly, and the connections are sufficiently well understood, so that reasonably close control over the money supply is feasible, given the will. I do not mean to say that the process would not involve much trial and some error but only that the errors need not be cumulative and could be corrected fairly promptly. The process involves technical problems of considerable complexity, but they are of a kind with which the System has much experience and for which the System has trained personnel.

The stock of money therefore seems to me the relevant magnitude in terms of which to formulate monetary rules and the behavior of which should be a criterion of policy performance. The question remains, what behavior of the stock of money should we seek to achieve either by instructing the monetary authorities to do so, or by designing a system under which the desired pattern would be produced automatically?

Some years ago, I suggested as one answer to this question a largely automatic framework that would link changes in the money supply to the state of the budget.[6] Surpluses in the budget would reduce the stock of money dollar for dollar and deficits would increase the stock of money dollar for dollar. The surpluses and deficits were themselves to result from the impact of changing economic conditions on a stable tax structure and a stable expenditure policy. The tax structure and expenditure policy were to be adjusted to the activities it was desired that government should undertake and not altered in reaction to cyclical movements—this is the "stabilizing budget policy" proposed at about the same time by the Committee for Economic Development.[7] This proposal would thus use the built-in flexibility of the federal budget as a means of producing counter-cyclical movements in the stock of money.

The research I have done since this proposal was published gives me no reason to doubt that it would work well; that it would provide a stable monetary background which would render major fluctuations well-nigh impossible, would not exacerbate minor fluctuations, and might even alleviate them. But I have become increasingly persuaded that the proposal is more sophisticated and complex than is necessary, that a much simpler rule would also produce highly satisfactory results and would have two great advantages: first, its simplicity would facilitate the public understanding and backing that is necessary if the rule is to provide an effective barrier to opportunistic "tinkering"; second, it would largely separate the monetary problem from the fiscal and hence would require less far-reaching reform over a narrower area.

The simpler rule is that the stock of money be increased at a fixed rate year-in and year-out without any variation in the rate of increase to meet cyclical needs. This rule could be adopted by the Reserve System itself. Alternatively, Congress could instruct the Reserve System to follow it. If it were adopted without any other changes in our monetary arrangements, the Reserve System would have much discretion in the precise techniques used to increase the stock of money and it could achieve the objective only with an appreciable though not large margin of error—perhaps one-half to one percentage point. If the other changes I have recommended were made, the area of discretion would be narrowed radically and so would the margin of error.

To make the rule specific, we need (1) to define the stock of money to which it refers, (2) to state what the fixed rate of increase should be or how it should be determined, (3) to state what if any allowance should be made for intra-year or seasonal movements.

(1) I have heretofore used the term "the stock of money" as if it were self-evident. Of course it is not. There is a continuum of assets possessing in various degrees the qualities we attribute to the ideal construct of "money" and hence there is no unique way to draw a line separating "money" from "near-monies"; for different purposes or at different times it may be appropriate to draw this line at different points on the continuum. In our own research we have found the most useful concept to be one that includes currency held by the public plus adjusted demand deposits plus time deposits in commercial banks but excludes time deposits in mutual savings banks, shares in savings and

loan associations, and the like. The Reserve System has generally used the term "money" more narrowly, to include only currency and demand deposits, and many economists have used it more broadly, to include also time deposits in mutual savings banks. I am inclined myself to favor the concept we have used because it seems to be somewhat more closely related empirically to income and other economic magnitudes than the other concepts and because it does not require classifying the deposit liabilities of individual institutions in terms of bookkeeping categories that permit much variation. But the evidence for this concept is certainly far from conclusive. More important, I do not believe it is vital which particular concept is chosen as long as first, it is at least as broad as currency plus adjusted demand deposits; second, a definite and clear-cut choice is made; and, third, the rate of increase chosen is adapted to the concept. The possible candidates for inclusion have had different secular rates of growth and are likely to continue to do so. They do not however vary radically with respect to one another over short periods and they would vary even less if some of my earlier suggestions were adopted, in particular, payment of interest on reserve balances with the Federal Reserve, and abolition of the present prohibition on the payment of interest on demand deposits and ceiling on the interest on time deposits.

(2) The rate of increase should be chosen so that on the average it could be expected to correspond with a roughly stable long-run level of final product prices. For the concept of money just recommended, namely, currency plus all commercial bank deposits, this would have required a rate of growth of slightly over 4% per year on the average of the past 90 years—something over 3% to allow for growth in output and 1% to allow for a secular decrease in velocity, which is to say for the increase in the stock of money per unit of output that the public has wished to hold as its real per capita income rose. To judge from this evidence, a rate of increase of 3 to 5% per year might be expected to correspond with a roughly stable price level for this particular concept of money. Since time deposits have grown in the past decade relative to demand deposits, and non-commercial bank time deposits relative to commercial, a somewhat lower rate of increase might be appropriate if a narrower definition were adopted, a somewhat higher rate, if a broader definition were adopted.

As with the definition, the particular rate of increase adopted seems to me less important than the adoption of a fixed rate provided only that the rate is somewhere in the range suggested and that it is adapted to the definition of money. A rate that turned out to be somewhat too high would mean a mild secular price rise, a rate that turned out to be somewhat too low, a mild secular price fall. Neither, it seems to me, would be serious. What is seriously disturbing to economic stability are rapid and sizable fluctuations in prices, not mild and steady secular movements in either direction. A fixed rate of increase in the stock of money would almost certainly rule out such rapid and sizable fluctuations, though it would not rule out mild cyclical or secular fluctuations, and it would give a firm basis for long range planning on the part of the public.

(3) I find the treatment of intra-year movements more puzzling. We now take for granted a seasonal movement in the stock of money and tend to assimilate it to other seasonal movements. Yet there is a crucial difference. The seasonal movement in the stock of money is a quasi-deliberate act of policy, not a product of climatic or similar circumstances. One initial objective of the Reserve System was to reduce seasonal fluctuations in interest rates. It has accomplished this objective by widening seasonal movements in the stock of money. I see no objection to seasonal variation in the stock of money, provided it is regular so that the public can adapt to it. On the other hand, neither do I see any objection to seasonal fluctuations in short-term interest rates. While the kind of pegging involved in eliminating seasonal fluctuations in interest rates has some special justifications, it is by no means free from the defects of other kinds of pegging. Moreover, there is no way to determine at all precisely what seasonal movement is required in the stock of money to eliminate a seasonal in interest rates. The actual seasonal that has been introduced into the stock of money has been sizable and has varied considerably from year to year. Hence, the proposal, which at first sight seems attractive, to apply a regular rate of increase to the seasonally adjusted stock of money, would involve introducing an essentially arbitrary element into the behavior of the stock of money—there is no seasonal to adjust until a decision is made what seasonal to introduce. My own tentative conclusion is that it would be preferable to dispense with seasonal adjustments and to adopt the rule that the actual stock of money should grow month by month at the predetermined rate. To avoid misunderstanding, let me note explicitly that this would be consistent with seasonal movements in currency and deposits separately, as long as they offset one another.

The proposal to increase the money stock at a fixed rate month-in and month-out is certainly simple. It is likely to strike many of you as also simple-minded. Surely, you will say, it is easy to do better. Surely, it would be better to "lean against the wind," in the expressive phrase of a Federal Reserve chairman, rather than to stand straight upright whichever way the wind is blowing. Some of my previous comments perhaps suggest that the matter is not so simple. We seldom in fact know which way the economic wind is blowing until several months after the event, yet to be effective, we need to know which way the wind is going to be blowing when the measures we take now will be effective, itself a variable date that may be a half year or a year or two years from now. Leaning today against next year's wind is hardly an easy task in the present state of meteorology.

Analogies aside, the historical record gives little basis for supposing that it is an easy task to do better than the simple rule I have suggested. Since at least the early 1920's, our monetary authorities have been trying to do just that; they have been trying to use monetary policy as an instrument for promoting stability. On the whole, the persons in charge of monetary policy have been as able, public spirited, and far-sighted a group as one could reasonably hope to have in such positions, though of course there have been some exceptions in both directions, and they have been served by a research staff that has numbered some of our leading monetary scholars and has maintained a high standard of technical excellence. Yet over this period as a whole, I doubt that many, if any, informed students of monetary affairs would disagree with the judgment that the actual behavior of the money stock has clearly been decidedly worse than the behavior that would have been produced by the simple rule—and this is true even if we leave out the war-time periods when the simple rule would almost surely have been departed from and perhaps rightly so.

The simple rule would have avoided the excessive expansion of the stock of money from 1919 to 1920 and the sharp contraction thereafter, the fairly mild but steady deflationary pressure of the later 1920's, the collapse of the stock of money from 1929 to 1933, the rather rapid rise thereafter, and the sharp decline in the course of the 1937–38 recession. In the period since World War II, the simple rule would have produced a lower rate of growth in the stock of money until the end of 1946 than was in fact realized, almost the same rate of growth during 1947, a faster rate of growth from sometime in 1947 to the end of 1949, which is to say, throughout the closing phases of the 1946–48 expansion and the whole of the 1948–49 contraction. The simple rule would have produced about the same rate of growth in the stock of money as was realized on the average from 1950 to early or mid-1953; a higher rate from then to mid-1954, or throughout most of the 1953–54 recession; about the same rate as was experienced from mid-1954 to mid-1955; a somewhat higher rate from then until the end of 1957; especially in the last half of 1957, after the 1957–58 contraction got under way; a lower rate than experienced in the first half of 1958, and about the same as the rate actually experienced from then to mid-1959.

The striking improvements in the behavior of the stock of money that would have been produced by the simple rule are for the inter-war period and for the major fluctuations of that period. It is these that make me so confident that informed students would render a nearly unanimous verdict in favor of the simple rule for the period as a whole. But, rule or no rule, changes in the monetary structure—notably federal insurance of bank deposits, the altered asset structure of banks, and the altered role of gold—and changes in the attitudes of the monetary authorities—notably their heightened sensitivity to contractions—render a repetition of major mistakes like those made during the inter-war period highly unlikely. It is nearly inconceivable that the monetary authorities would now permit the money stock to decline by one-third, as it did from 1929–33, or even by nearly 4% in 10 months, as it did in 1937. It is no doubt a merit of the rule that it provides insurance against such major mistakes but it may plausibly be argued that other factors have already provided adequate insurance—though I would be tempted to add that new mistakes are legion and insurance against major mistakes differing in kind from those in the past, in particular against unduly large increases in the money supply, is well worth while.

For the period since World War II, the contrast is not nearly so clear or sharp. The monetary authorities have followed a policy that has produced a behavior of the money supply very close to its hypothetical behavior under the rule, far closer than between the wars. In consequence, a finer criterion of performance is required to judge the desirability or undesirability of such discrepancies as there are, and this is true also for the milder discrepancies in the earlier period. My own judgment is that even for these, the rule would have produced clearly superior results, but I cannot be so sure that this judgment would be widely shared as I am for the period as a whole.

To supplement my own personal judgment, I tried to devise some objective way of grading actual performance relative to hypothetical performance under the rule. The attempt failed. The reason why it failed is, I think, most instructive. It is because the attempt to give operational meaning to "better and worse performance" revealed that such formulae as "leaning against the wind" or "countercyclical changes in the money supply," with which there might be widespread agreement, have no unambiguous specific content. I suspect that this is the only reason there is such widespread agreement. Each person can read his own content into these vague statements. If one tries to translate them into specific criteria that can be used to judge actual performance *ex post,* let alone to guide performance in the future, he finds that there are a variety of alternative translations, no one of which is fully satisfactory to any one person and on no one of which would there be anything like general agreement. In answer to the question whether it would be possible to do better than the simple rule, a majority of informed students might say "yes." Further probing would, however, reveal wide variety in the specific alternative policy regarded as "better." If each of these were made as explicit as the simple rule, I doubt that there would be anything like general assent to any one.

I can best elaborate on these remarks by describing briefly my attempts. Month-by-month, I recorded whether the growth in the seasonally adjusted actual money supply was higher or lower than the growth that would have been produced by a steady 4% rate of growth. I then tried to classify the difference as in the "right" or "wrong" direction according to an objective policy criterion.

The first criterion I tried was a simple translation of "leaning against the wind," namely, that the stock of money should grow at a slower than average rate during business expansions and at a higher than average rate during business contractions. By this criterion, for eight complete peacetime reference cycles from March 1919 to April 1958 (excluding the World War II cycle from June 1938 to October 1945), actual policy was in the "right" direction in 155 months, in the "wrong" direction in 226 months; so actual policy was "better" than the rule in 41% of the months. For the period after World War II alone, the results were only slightly more favorable to actual policy according to this criterion: policy was in the "right" direction in 71 months, in the "wrong" direction in 79 months, so actual policy was better than the rule in 47% of the months.

Even if the policy criterion could be accepted, numbers like these would not be an adequate measure of performance for three very different reasons. First, and least serious given a sufficiently long span of time, they take no account of the magnitude of the difference, only the direction. Second, and more serious, they treat each month separately, taking no account of the time sequence of deviations, and therefore neglect completely cumulative effects—a given number of deviations in the "wrong" direction could have very different consequences according as they were clustered or dispersed in time. Third, and most basic, suppose the results were less extreme and that actual policy were in the "right" direction 50% of the time. Would that mean a dead heat between the two alternative policies? Not at all. The alternative to the rule involves variability in the rate of change of the money supply; if the score is 50–50, this variability is simply a disturbance that introduces instability. Hence a 50–50 score would mean that the rule would be decidedly preferable—any alternative must be "better" much more than half the time in order to offset the harm it does through introducing random variability.[8]

The policy criterion cannot however be accepted. This is clear as soon as one goes beyond the overall results, and looks at the scoring of individual months. According to this criterion, a rate of growth higher than 4% is scored as in the wrong direction from March 1933 to May 1937. But this is absurd. Economic activity may have changed its direction of movement in March 1933 but it was still abnormally low. Surely a rule that calls for reversing policy toward "tightness" the moment a cyclical trough is reached is unsatisfactory—"ease" should be continued as long as conditions are depressed. Stating the counterpart for the peak reveals an inflationary asymmetry in reaction. There will be far less agreement that a "tight" policy should be continued beyond the peak so long as conditions are prosperous. If, however, we follow the logic both ways, we get an alternative translation of "leaning against the wind" to the effect that the money supply should grow at a slower than average rate during periods when economic conditions are "above" normal and at a faster than average rate when economic conditions are "below" normal. For simplicity, I treated the period from mid-expansion to mid-contraction as "above" normal and from mid-contraction to mid-expansion as "below" normal. By this criterion, actual policy scored much higher, being in the right direction in 56%

of 377 peacetime months for the period as a whole, and in 58% of 149 months after World War II.[9]

Once again, examination of the month-by-month scoring raises serious doubts. In the Great Depression, for example, a less than normal rate of growth is scored as in the "right" direction from August 1929 all the way to the middle of 1931; and again more recently, from the cyclical peak in November 1948 through April 1949; and from the peak in July 1953 through January 1954. Some improvement might be made by adopting a less mechanical definition of "above" and "below" normal, such as the relation of income or industrial production, or some index of business conditions to its trend, or unemployment or prices to some "normal" level. But which should it be?

The two criteria so far described agree in classifying as "right" a less than normal rate of growth during the second half of expansion and a more than normal rate during the second half of contraction. This greatest common denominator of the two criteria is of course useless for future policy; it can, however, be used as at least a partial basis for judging past performance. By this third criterion, actual policy was in the "right" direction 45% of 183 peacetime months for the period as a whole, 55% of 75 months since the end of World War II.[10]

But even this common denominator is not unexceptionable. Once account is taken of the lag between monetary action and its effects, it is not at all clear that it is desirable to continue a lower-than-average rate of growth right up to the cyclical peak and a higher-than-average rate of growth up to the cyclical trough. If we could, might it not be desirable to ease monetary conditions before the peak and start tightening before the trough? Once again, reactions are likely to display an inflationary asymmetry—we readily agree at the peak, but many are likely to question the desirability of tightening before the trough is reached.

Still another range of possibilities is opened up by allowing not only for leads but also for a modified "needs of trade" argument. It has been argued that meeting a contraction arising from non-monetary forces with a larger than normal rate of increase in the money supply floods the market with liquidity, encourages investment in housing and other areas that is not viable in the longer run, and stimulates "speculation." In these ways, it creates difficulties for the future. Reverse phenomena are said to occur in the expansion. On this view, the appropriate behavior of the money supply is to move with the wind but only mildly; to grow at a slower rate than normal during at least the early stages of contraction and at a faster rate than normal during at least part of the expansion.

The diversity and ambiguity concealed by the phrase "countercyclical monetary policy" itself raises something of a puzzle. How is it that there can yet be wide consensus in retrospective judgments of the major fluctuations? The answer, I conjecture, is that these involved *large* movements and that whatever the precise pattern specified, there would be general agreement that the rate of growth of the stock of money should not deviate far from some long-run average rate of growth. If this be so, then the simple rule I have proposed itself embodies an element that is common to most views about the appropriate behavior of the stock of money, is itself something of a greatest common denominator.

But whether this be the explanation or not, one thing seems clear. There is not currently any well-defined alternative to the rule I have suggested that would command wide assent, unless it be "let the Federal Reserve System do it"; and even for this alternative, there is no well-defined criterion with which there would be wide agreement for judging *ex post* whether "they" have done "it" well or poorly.

In summing up this discussion of the appropriate behavior of the money stock, I am tempted to paraphrase what Colin Clark once wrote about the case for free trade. Like other academicians, I am accustomed to being met with the refrain, "It's all right in theory but it won't work in practice." Aside from the questionable logic of the remark in general, in this instance almost the reverse of what is intended is true. There is little to be said in theory for the rule that the money supply should grow at a constant rate. The case for it is entirely that it would work in practice. There are persuasive theoretical grounds for desiring to vary the rate of growth to offset other factors. The difficulty is that, in practice, we do not know when to do so and by how much. In practice, therefore, deviations from the simple rule have been destabilizing rather than the reverse.

I should like to emphasize that I do not regard steady growth in the money stock as the be-all and end-all of monetary policy for all time. It is a rule that has much to recommend it in the present state of our knowledge. It would avoid the major mistakes that have marred our past record. It would assure long-run stability in the purchasing power of the dollar. But I should hope that as we operated under it we would accumulate more evidence and learn to understand more fully the workings of the monetary mechanism. As we did so, we could perhaps devise still better rules for controlling the stock of money that could command widespread professional support and public understanding.

CONCLUSION

In the course of this book, I have made a series of sweeping suggestions for reforming our monetary and banking arrangements (a summary is appended). Let us suppose that reforms along these lines were adopted. What might one reasonably expect from them?

The major gains would be, first, effective insurance against major monetary disturbances; second, a notable reduction in short-term monetary uncertainty and instability; third, a wider scope for private initiative and enterprise in the allocation of capital. The first would contribute to, if not effectively guarantee, the avoidance of those major economic disturbances that from time to time have threatened to tear our social fabric asunder. The second would promote a greater degree of stability in short-run movements in economic activity and thus contribute to what has become one of the major aims of national economic policy. The third would expand the area of economic freedom and promote a more efficient utilization of our resources, whether for current consumption or to increase our rate of growth.

These would be no mean accomplishments. But they would not provide a panacea for economic problems. Money is important, but only, in John Stuart Mill's words, "as a contrivance for sparing time and labour."[11] There are other sources of uncertainty and instability. No doubt they will continue to produce recurrent fluctuations in economic activity and from time to time will give rise to more serious problems of economic adjustment. Monetary policy is but one segment of total governmental policy let alone of the far wider range of private and public economic arrangements that affect the course of events. And even if we could improve governmental policy in other areas as much as our limited knowledge and understanding would permit, some uncertainty and instability would remain. After all, uncertainty and instability are unavoidable concomitants of progress and change. They are one face of a coin of which the other is freedom.

SUMMARY OF RECOMMENDATIONS

A. WITH RESPECT TO FEDERAL RESERVE SYSTEM:

1. Instruct the System to use its open market powers to produce a 4% per year rate of growth in the total of currency held by the public and adjusted deposits in commercial banks. The System should be instructed to keep the rate of growth as steady as it can week by week and month by month and to introduce no seasonal movement in the money stock.
2. Repeal present requirement that the Reserve System must maintain a gold reserve equal to 25% of its liabilities.
3. Require the Reserve System to pay interest to member banks on its deposit liabilities at a rate designed to be the same as the market yield on short-term government securities. Require the System to charge at cost for check-clearing or other services to member banks.
4. Repeal present control by the System over interest rates that member banks may pay on time deposits and present prohibition of interest payments by member banks on demand deposits.
5. Repeal present control over margin requirements on securities.
6. Repeal present power of the System to make loans to member banks, to discount paper for them, and to make loans to private individuals, corporations, or non-federal public bodies. This would eliminate any necessity for the System to establish discount rates or eligibility requirements.
7. Impose a set of fines on member banks for discrepancies between required and actual reserves.
8. Repeal present power of the System to vary reserve requirements of member banks (see also C1 and C1a below).
9. Give Reserve System power to issue its own securities, particularly if debt management functions are assigned to System.

B. WITH RESPECT TO THE TREASURY:

1. Eliminate present debt management by Treasury. Require Treasury to acquire funds it needs from Reserve System and deposit surpluses with Reserve System. This would concentrate debt management in one agency.
1a. Alternatively, if this step is not taken, modify Treasury debt management as follows:

(1) Reduce kinds of issues offered to two—a short-term bill and a longer-term security, say an 8-year bond.

(2) Issue both securities at regular and frequent intervals, preferably weekly, if not bi-weekly or monthly.

(3) Announce the amount to be issued periodically as long in advance as possible and vary the amount smoothly from date to date.

(4) Sell both issues solely at public auction and use an auction method under which all purchasers pay the same price.

(5) As far as possible, rely on either deposits in commercial banks or in Reserve Banks for Treasury transactions, avoiding shifts between them.

2. Eliminate present commitment to buy and sell gold at a fixed price of $35 an ounce. Permit foreign exchange rates to be determined in the free market without Treasury intervention.

3. Eliminate present provisions for purchase of silver, retire silver certificates, and dispose of present silver stocks at a regular rate over the course of a decade or so.

4. Retire U.S. notes and authorize issue of Federal Reserve notes in small denominations, so that hand-to-hand currency will consist exclusively of Federal Reserve notes and coin.

C. WITH RESPECT TO COMMERCIAL BANKS:

1. Require banks accepting deposits subject to recall on demand or to transfer by check to keep reserves equal to 100% of their deposit liabilities whether demand or time in the form of either currency in vault or interest-bearing deposits with the Reserve System. Permit completely free entry in the deposit banking business.

1a. Alternatively, if this step is not taken, revise present reserve requirements so as to make them uniform for all banks and all classes of deposits, with reserves being defined to include both vault cash and interest-bearing deposits with the Reserve System. This would mean eliminating present distinctions between central reserve, reserve city, and country banks, and between demand and time deposits.

2. Repeal present prohibition on the payment of interest on demand deposits and present limitations on interest rates that may be paid on time deposits (see A4 above for member banks).

Notes

Chapter One

1 The first three paragraphs are adapted from my introductory statement in testimony before the Joint Economic Committee on May 25, 1959. See *Hearings on Employment, Growth, and Price Levels*, Part 4, The Influence on Prices of Changes in the Effective Supply of Money (United States Government Printing Office, Washington, 1959), pp. 606–07.

2 U.S. Congress, Joint Economic Committee:
Hearings before the Subcommittee on Monetary, Credit and Fiscal Policies, 1949, Senator Paul H. Douglas, Chairman.
Statements to the Subcommittee on Monetary, Credit and Fiscal Policies, 1949.
Report of the Subcommittee on Monetary, Credit and Fiscal Policies, 1950.
Hearings before the Subcommittee on General Credit Control and Debt Management, 1952, Rep. Wright Patman, Chairman.
Monetary Policy and the Management of the Public Debt. Parts 1 and 2, 1952.
Report of the Subcommittee on General Credit Control and Debt Management, 1952.

3 U.S. Congress, Joint Economic Committee:
Hearings before the Subcommittee on Economic Stabilization:
United States Monetary Policy, Recent Thinking and Experience, 1954, Senator Ralph E. Flanders, Chairman.
U.S. Congress, Senate Committee on Finance, Senator Harry F. Byrd, Chairman:
Investigation of the Financial Condition of the United States, Parts 1–6, Hearings, 1957–1958.
Investigation of the Financial Condition of the United States: Compendium, 1958.

103

U.S. Congress, Joint Economic Committee, Rep. Wright Patman, Chairman:
The Relationship of Prices to Economic Stability and Growth:
Compendium, 1958.
The Relationship of Prices to Economic Stability and Growth:
Hearings, 1958.
U.S. Congress, Joint Economic Committee, Senator Paul H. Douglas, Chairman:
Hearings on Employment, Growth and Price Levels
Part 1. The American Economy: Problems and Prospects, 1959.
Part 2. Historical and Comparative Rates of Production, Productivity, and Prices, 1959.
Part 3. Historical and Comparative Rates of Labor Force, Employment and Unemployment, 1959.
Part 4. The Influence on Prices of Changes in the Effective Supply of Money, 1959.
Part 5. International Influences on the American Economy, 1959.
Parts 6 A, B, C. The Government's Management of its Monetary, Fiscal, and Debt Operations, 1959.
Part 7. The Effect of Monopolistic and Quasi-Monopolistic Practices upon Prices, Profits, Production, and Employment, 1959.
Part 8. The Effect of Increases in Wages, Salaries and the Prices of Personal Services together with Union and Professional Practices upon Prices, Profits, Production, and Employment, 1959.
Parts 9 A, B. Constructive Suggestions for Reconciling and Simultaneously Obtaining the Three Objectives of Maximum Employment, an Adequate Rate of Growth and Substantial Stability of the Price Level, 1959.

4 *United States Monetary Policy,* Neil H. Jacoby, ed. (The American Assembly: Columbia University, December 1958).

5 Incidentally, under such a standard, an increased demand for money would be a demand for a commodity and hence an indirect demand for the factors of production used in producing it; hence, unemployment arising out of a liquidity trap of the Keynesian type would be impossible. The tendency for earlier writers to reason implicitly in terms of a commodity standard is, I believe, one reason why the liquidity trap did not make its appearance earlier as a potential source of disequilibrium and unemployment.

6 If we suppose that technological change does not affect the relative costs of production of the monetary commodity and other goods and services, and that the monetary commodity is produced under conditions of roughly constant relative costs in the long run for the range of output in question, then the equilibrium output will be that which would keep product prices in terms of the monetary commodity constant. If output were smaller than this, costs of production of the monetary commodity would fall relative to its (constant) nominal selling price and it would pay to expand output and conversely. For the United States, past experience suggests that the stock of money would have to grow by about 4% a year to keep product prices

roughly constant—3% to allow for growth in aggregate output and 1% to allow for the increase in the real stock of money per unit of output that has accompanied the growth of per capita income in the past. Four percent of end-of-1958 money stock, defined as including currency held by the public, adjusted demand deposits, and time deposits in commercial banks, is about $8 billion which is about 2½ % of estimated net national product for calendar 1958.

Of course, differential technological change would affect the actual outcome but there is no saying in which direction.

7 A full analysis of our monetary experience, for the 90-year period since the Civil War, will be presented in a National Bureau monograph by Anna Schwartz and myself. The summary that follows rests heavily on this analysis.

8 See Bray Hammond, *Banks and Politics in America,* from the Revolution to the Civil War (Princeton, 1957), pp. 459–77, 503–13.

Had Biddle's project succeeded, he would have been regarded as a great public benefactor rather than the subject of widespread obloquy. His failure was by no means inevitable. It was the result of continued world-wide depression and an associated decline in the world price of cotton.

9 See George Macesich, *Monetary Disturbances in the United States, 1834–45,* unpublished Ph.D. thesis at the University of Chicago (June, 1958).

The Bank made several attempts at resumption and did not finally close its doors until 1841.

10 See James K. Kindahl, *The Economics of Resumption: The United States, 1865–1879,* unpublished Ph.D. thesis at the University of Chicago (August, 1958).

11 The numerical values are .0587 for 1867 through 1914; .0848 for 1914 through 1958. These standard deviations are computed from the first differences of the natural logarithms of the money stock for successive Junes. For the earlier years, the June value was obtained by linear interpolation of the absolute money stock figures for the closest months for which the figures were available.

12 The numerical value for these thirty-three years is .0710.

Chapter Two

1 See Lloyd W. Mints, *A History of Banking Theory* (Chicago, 1945), especially Chapters XI and XII.

2 Algebraically, let C = currency held by the public
D = deposits held by the public
R = vault cash plus commercial bank deposits with Reserve Banks
M = money supply
H = high-powered money

Then
$$M = C + D,$$
$$H = C + R,$$

$$\frac{M}{H} = \frac{C+D}{C+R} = \frac{\dfrac{C}{D}+1}{\dfrac{C}{D}+\dfrac{R}{D}}.$$

Hence
$$M = H \cdot \frac{\dfrac{C}{D}+1}{\dfrac{C}{D}+\dfrac{R}{D}}.$$

Note that the various terms must be defined consistently. For example, if D includes deposits in mutual savings banks, then their vault cash must be included in R; if D excludes deposits in mutual savings banks, their vault cash must be included in C. If D includes all deposits in commercial banks, as we shall suppose throughout, then R includes all high-powered money held by commercial banks. If D is restricted to demand deposits, then either R must still be defined to include all high-powered money held by commercial banks, in which case $\dfrac{D}{R}$ is not a very meaningful ratio, or the high-powered money held by commercial banks must be regarded as composed of two parts, one held in connection with demand deposits, the other in connection with time deposits; only the first included in R, and the second included in C.

3 The complete avoidance of all loans to member banks would require a change in methods of clearing checks, since present methods involve a loan at zero interest to member banks in the form of Federal Reserve "float." For simplicity, I shall ignore this problem. Float is a source of considerable day-to-day and week-to-week variability in Federal Reserve credit outstanding, so that a full reform along the line I am suggesting would require some attention to it. At the same time, it is an automatic resultant of the method of clearing checks, not a source of credit that is manipulated either by the System or member banks, or could easily be.

4 For simplicity, I am assuming that Treasury balances with the Federal Reserve are not subject to Reserve control. In practice of course, through cooperation with the Treasury, the amount of high-powered money in the hands of the public could also be changed by a shift of Treasury deposits between commercial banks and the Federal Reserve. (See page 55.)

5 A striking example is Roose's exhaustive, and otherwise excellent, analysis of the 1937–38 contraction. Though Roose is highly eclectic in his approach, he devotes no attention whatsoever to the effects of the Reserve System's policy on the stock of money, considering only its effects on market interest rates. Kenneth D. Roose, *The Economics of Recession and Revival* (New Haven, 1954), pp. 101–02.

6 In these remarks I have neglected one element of the specific historical context in order to stress the part of general validity. The System was at the

time deliberately avoiding open-market operations. It kept its holdings of government securities almost perfectly constant for years except for net purchases of nearly $100 million in April 1937 induced by the reactions to the reserve requirement changes. In the absence of the power to vary reserve requirements it might of course have followed a different policy but it seems unlikely, in view of other attendant circumstances, that it would have done so.

Chapter Three

1 A source of confusion not touched on above is the failure to distinguish sharply two questions: the kinds of securities issued and who buys them. It is logically valid to argue that a given volume of securities is more inflationary (or less deflationary) if short-term than long-term in part because it raises short-term interest rates, and thereby induces banks to maintain a lower ratio of reserves to deposits. But this effect is independent of who buys the securities; it will follow even if none are bought by the banks, since the rise in short-term rates on governments will be accompanied by a corresponding rise on comparable other securities.

Another detailed point requiring attention is the effect of the system of spaced "calls" for transfer of Treasury deposits to the Federal Reserve referred to in the next paragraph in the text. This may make Treasury deposits more attractive than other deposits because of the knowledge that they will not be withdrawn without notice, and hence lead banks to purchase Treasury securities which give rise to such deposits on terms at which they would not be willing to buy other securities. However, these effects are purely nominal and do not affect the main point. Until the Treasury transfers the deposit, it is in effect simply paying a fee for an advance commitment by the bank. Economically speaking, the sale is not effectively consummated until a transfer is called for and at this point, the analysis in the text applies in full.

2 For currency, this would require retiring U.S. notes, demonetizing silver, and retiring silver certificates. In addition, the Reserve System would have to be authorized to issue Federal Reserve notes in denominations of $1 and $2. The smallest denomination now authorized is $5.

3 By the Act of March 27, 1942, the Reserve Banks were authorized to purchase government obligations directly from the Treasury with a limit of $5 billion imposed on the aggregate amount held at any one time. This power was originally granted through December 1944; but has since been regularly renewed.

Before 1935, direct purchases from and sales to the Treasury by Federal Reserve Banks were permitted by section 14(b) of the Federal Reserve Act, but section 206 of the Banking Act of 1935 limited the purchase of direct and guaranteed government obligations to the open market.

4 See *Treasury-Federal Reserve Study of the Government Securities Market*, Part 1 (July 1959) and "The Government Securities Market," *Federal Reserve Bulletin*, August 1959, pp. 860–81.

5 An interesting piece of evidence is the change in maturity implicit in

the elimination of the bond support program after the Reserve-Treasury Accord of 1951. Prior to this, all nominally long-term securities had been effectively demand obligations. Thereafter, they became long-term securities in fact as well as name. This was surely a drastic change. The effect was to increase the demand for money by something like 2 or 3%—the money stock rose some 6% in the year following the Accord without a price rise, whereas about 3 to 4% per year seems the amount that was subsequently and in the long past as well consistent with stable prices.

6 For example, a bidder might submit one bid offering to buy X_1 dollars of securities at any price below P_1; X_2 dollars at a lower price, P_2, implying that he would buy at least $X_1 + X_2$ at a price of P_2 or less; and so on for other prices.

7 See especially, "The Government's Management of its Monetary, Fiscal, and Debt Operations," Part 6A of *Hearings on Employment, Growth, and Price Levels* before Joint Economic Committee (Washington, 1959), pp. 1150–53. Since the lectures on which this book is based were given, the alternative auction procedure proposed in the text has been independently suggested by Deane Carson, "Treasury Open Market Operations," *Review of Economics and Statistics,* Nov. 1959, p. 441.

8 Henry C. Simons, "A Positive Program for Laissez Faire: Some Proposals for a Liberal Economic Policy," in his *Economic Policy for A Free Society* (Chicago, 1948), pp. 62–5 (first published as "Public Policy Pamphlet, No. 15, ed. Harry D. Gideonse (Chicago, 1934); Lloyd W. Mints, *Monetary Policy for a Competitive Society* (New York, 1950), pp. 186–87. Albert G. Hart, "The 'Chicago Plan' of Banking Reform," *Review of Economic Studies,* 2 (1935), pp. 104–16. Reprinted in Friedrich A. Lutz and Lloyd W. Mints (eds.), *Readings in Monetary Theory* (New York, 1951), pp. 437–56.

9 Banks were required to deposit as security for notes, government bonds equal in face value before March 1900 to 111%, thereafter to 100% of the value of the notes issued. From 1874 on, they also had to deposit a 5% redemption fund.

10 An alternative way to eliminate governmental intervention that Gary Becker has persuaded me has merit is to move in the opposite direction, to keep currency issue as a governmental monopoly, but to permit "free" deposit banking, without any requirements about reserves, or supervision over assets or liabilities, and with a strict *caveat emptor* policy. It seems highly possible that under modern conditions, with the much increased financial sophistication of the community, urban concentration of population, and speedy communication and transmission of information, such a banking system would raise no serious problems of the kind that not very different systems did more than a century ago. Such a system would avoid one social cost of the 100% reserve system—the prohibition of some arrangements among individuals that they find mutually advantageous. It would not, however, solve the problem of "inherent instability."

11 The objections to the creation of additional debt to finance deficits

will appear more clearly when account is taken of the proposal to pay interest on reserves. The use of this device then means letting the amount of interest payment, and the associated taxes to be levied, be determined by the rate at which it is desired to increase the stock of money. It is not clear that this is the relevant criterion. The purchase of other assets would avoid this problem, since they would yield income. But this involves putting the government into the banking business.

One way to resolve this problem would be to achieve the objectives aimed at by paying interest on deposits by holding the stock of money per capita constant and thus producing a declining price level of final products (see below). This solution would be admirable if frictions of adjustment and rigidities in prices and wages could be largely neglected. They constitute the chief argument against it.

It is interesting, though not perhaps surprising, that this issue should be connected with the issue of the desirable long-run behavior of prices.

12 See Mints, *op. cit.*, p. 186, and especially George S. Tolley, "Providing for Growth of the Money Supply," *Journal of Political Economy*, Dec. 1957, p. 477.

13 *Ibid.*, pp. 477–84.

14 Note that this argument does not apply to a commodity currency because such a currency requires real resources for its production.

15 For example, Treasury notes of 1812–15, in denominations from $20 to $100; the Treasury notes of 1837–43 and 1860; during the Civil War, both legal tender notes (one-year, 5% Treasury notes of 1863; two-year, 5% Treasury notes of 1863; compound interest notes) and government obligations not legal tender (certificates of indebtedness and three-year Treasury notes bearing 7.3% interest).

16 "Why the American Economy is Depression-Proof," *Nationalekonomiska Föreningens Forhadinger*, 1954 (Stockholm, 1954), pp. 60–1.

Chapter Four

1 (New York, 1924), esp. Ch. IV.

2 See "The Case for Flexible Exchange Rates," in *Essays in Positive Economics* (Chicago, 1953), pp. 157–203.

3 *Journal of Political Economy*, XLIV (1936), pp. 1–30; reprinted in Henry C. Simons, *Economic Policy for a Free Society* (Chicago, 1948), pp. 160–83.

4 Federal Reserve Act, Section 14, paragraph 5. The Banking Act of 1933 changed the language of Section 14, paragraph 5, to specify "the maintenance of sound credit conditions, and the accommodation of commerce, industry and agriculture" as a guide to Federal Reserve action.

5 Even the *Annual Report* for 1933 comments in this vein on the Banking Holiday: "The ability of the Federal Reserve banks to meet enormous demands for currency during the crisis demonstrated the effectiveness of the country's currency system under the Federal Reserve Act. . . . The crisis

of February and March 1933, therefore, was not a currency crisis but a banking crisis, and was occasioned not by a shortage of currency but by loss of confidence in the solvency of banks and by a depreciation in bank assets consequent upon the drop in prices of all classes of property caused by the depression." And again, later in the same report, "It is difficult to say what the course of the depression would have been had the Federal Reserve System not pursued a policy of liberal open-market purchases." (*Twentieth Annual Report*, pp. 1,20–21.)

6 See "A Monetary and Fiscal Framework for Economic Stability," *American Economic Review*, XXXVIII (June 1948), 254–64; reprinted in my *Essays in Positive Economics*, pp. 133–56; also in Friedrich A. Lutz and Lloyd W. Mints, selection committee of the American Economic Association, *Readings in Monetary Theory* (1951), pp. 369–93.

7 Committee for Economic Development, *Taxes and the Budget: A Program for Prosperity in a Free Economy* (November 1947).

8 For a fuller analysis of this problem, see my "The Effects of a Full-Employment Policy on Economic Stability: A Formal Analysis," *Essays in Positive Economics*, pp. 117–32.

9 The periods covered are from Nov.–Dec., 1918 to Nov.–Dec., 1957, excluding Nov.–Dec., 1937 to June, 1945. The numerical results are 210 months in the right direction to 167 in the wrong for the whole period; 87 to 62 for the period after June 1945.

10 Actual scores were 83 out of 183 in the "right" direction for the period as a whole; 41 out of 75 for postwar period.

11 *Principles of Political Economy*, Ashley Edition (New York, 1929), p. 488.